Mindful Devotions:
a 40-Day Journey Through the Bible

KAREN OPENSHAW
&
CHRIS EDMONDSON

Published by Fresh Expressions
www.freshexpressions.org.uk

With thanks to Karen Markham
for the cover image.
Karen is an artist from the northwest of
England who splits her time between
art and working in a primary school.
You can find her artwork at:
www.facebook.com/karenmarkhamartist
www.instagram.com/karenmarkhamartist

CONTENTS

Foreword

Mindfulness is both a buzzword and misunderstood! A key question to ask is what is the origin of mindfulness? As mindfulness is our God-given capacity for attention, awareness, and bringing things to our attention (remembering), then God is the origin of mindfulness. It is then helpful to ask what is the purpose of being mindful, why has God given us capacities of attention, awareness, and remembering? God is mindful of us (Psalm 8) as Chris and Karen remind us. We are made in his image and are, therefore, called to be mindful of and attentive to God, our own self, others, and the created world, as well as our social context.

Our spirituality and mental health do overlap and influence each other. Mindfulness for health in secular psychology is therapeutic in intention. Here in this devotional book the emphasis is on spiritual formation. However, mindfulness is good for you and so every aspect of our lives can be impacted by our spiritual life, including our wellbeing.

This is a book of wisdom, and the best form of contemplation always leads to action. This is how the authors have structured each day's reflection – contemplation leading to action. The scriptural passages that have been chosen for us to feed on are full of goodness and truth. They have come out of the authors' own spiritual journeys with God.

It is important that Christians reclaim the word mindfulness, but also take their place at the table. Our contemplative wisdom stretches back two thousand years. We should not remove ourselves from the marketplace of mindfulness or allow ourselves to be squeezed out. Christian mindfulness, as mindfulness of God, is an important distinctive that has biblical and historical roots; but which needs recontextualising in our culture, which is asking spiritual questions – but not of us. This is a very significant missional opportunity which the authors have picked up on in their own holy noticing of the mission of God.

Basing each day around reflection and meditation on scripture (a form of Lectio Divina) leading to action is a foundational spiritual discipline which is given a freshness through the lens of mindfulness.

The mindful action for each day is not a formal meditation as might be found in secular mindfulness, but on some days, we are asked to pay attention to our breath which some may find difficult. If that's you then just find a different mindful action for that day.

It is important when we engage with secular mindfulness that we find trained teachers - as the authors advise.

If we live with a mental health condition, then it is helpful to ask our doctor if mindfulness is right for us. Christianity offers a different way of paying attention but that does not mean as we turn and face reality that we don't experience difficulties.

At its heart, mindfulness, of God and in particular gazing at the face of Christ, is about transformation into Christlikeness (2 Corinthians 3:18). It is about receiving as a graced gift, fullness of life in the midst of suffering. Not only can you use this book to bring liberation to your own life, but also it could be a gift for others who are on your heart.

Rev Dr Shaun Lambert (October 2022)

Introduction

After the publication of *Mindfulness as Mission Gift* we felt we wanted to create something to enable Christians, and those who are open to learning more about Jesus, to carve out a period of time to devote to living more mindfully and to be mindful of the presence of God. We wanted it to be simple enough to slot into the busyness of the day yet engaging enough to act as a spiritual discipline such as during a season like Lent. We have unpacked some of the scriptures about mindfulness we quote in our previous publication and also added others. It's amazing how the more we read the Bible the more we notice references to God's mindfulness of us.

We have invited other contributions so that there are different 'voices' in the text, and we are delighted to share from key people in the world of Christian mindfulness, some of whom we quote in MAMG. Among these are applied theologians, practitioners, and mindfulness experts, along with those who, like me (Karen), have discovered that the practice of mindfulness of God has been personally transformational. With contributions from different theological traditions and perspectives we especially loved two of our contributors' different approaches to Psalm 46:10, and we hope you do too.

Each day there is a verse (or verses) of scripture which we believe encapsulates either God's mindfulness of us or the mindfulness of Jesus. Our vision is that this will be used in a similar way to a Lectio Divina, and our hope is that this will not simply be an exercise of the mind but for it to feel experiential, to filter down to your heart and soul. There is a short contextual reflection, a mindful thought, a mindful action to take into the day and a prayer. There is space too for you to journal your own reflections or perhaps draw any images that come to you.

We hope this encourages and blesses you on your journey;

and that it enables you to be more mindful of the presence of God, the love of Christ, and the need for compassion for yourself and toward others.

Prayer to pray daily
based on the Kindness Meditation*

We suggest that you begin each day of reflections with the following prayer. It has been adapted from the kindness meditation* which is to be found on the next page

Loving God, we live in a broken world, but we know that you want good things for us, your children.

Thank you for your mindfulness of us.

We pray that you would keep us safe, protecting us from inner and outer danger and harm.

Free us from mental suffering or distress. Help us to be aware of our thoughts and to give them to you.

Renew our mental health and physical strength each morning as you've promised.

Help us to live out our lives loving you, our neighbours, and ourselves.

May you fill us with your Holy Spirit and shine through us to your glory.

In all circumstances make us joy filled people of peace, always mindful of your presence in us.

In Jesus' name we pray, Amen.

Karen Openshaw & Julie Macauley 2022

*Kindness meditation

May I be free from inner and outer danger and harm
May I be safe and protected
May I be free of mental suffering or distress
May I be happy
May I be healthy
May I be strong
May I be able to live in this world happily,
peacefully, joyfully and with ease.[1]

---

[1] https://cac.org/daily-meditations/all-will-be-well-weekly-summary-2021-04-10/ - accessed 31 Aug 22.

'How to Use' Guide

Whilst we don't want to be prescriptive, we thought it might be helpful to suggest how to use these mindful devotions.

Alone

You could use them as a spiritual discipline during a period such as Advent or Lent, to immerse yourself in each day. Equally each devotional does stand alone so could be used on an 'ad hoc' basis.

In a small group setting

With other Christians:
They could be used as a resource - possibly in a home or bible study group - for Christians interested in learning more about how to be mindful and to discover the many threads of mindfulness contained within the pages of the Bible.

In a mindfulness group:
They could also be used with mindfulness practitioners who are open and curious to learn how mindfulness and Christianity are connected.

Let's begin...

First, find a space where you are unlikely to be interrupted.

Find a comfortable position. Just notice how you are feeling. Pause...

Pray

Read the prayer (on page 4) which we have based upon the kindness meditation.

Scripture

Now read the scripture - preferably out loud. Engage with what you are reading. Perhaps you might even imagine yourself there?

Reflection

Before engaging with the reflection take some time to just pause again - perhaps re-read the passage.

Thought

Now read the thought. What does this say to you?

Action

Next read the action. Do you need to write it down or make a note? Commit to undertaking the action over the course of the day to come, or the following day if you read the devotion at night. But show yourself kindness and self-compassion if this doesn't happen.

Prayer

Read the final prayer - preferably out loud.

Your space

Exactly what it says. This is for you to use how you feel prompted. You may wish to use the space to draw an image, doodle or write down your thoughts.

Some Final Words Before the Devotions

We want to stress that neither of us are qualified mindfulness teachers - though some of our contributors are. This is not a secular mindfulness publication - it is a devotional written from a mindfully Christian perspective. If, through the insights we share, you are drawn to undertake a Mindfulness Based Stress Reduction course there are many accredited courses available. There is also now an overarching body for Mindfulness practitioners (BAMBA.) We include a resource list for further reading particularly for those interested in Christian Mindfulness.

We also commend as a secular mindfulness book "Mindfulness: A Practical Guide to Finding Peace in a Frantic World" by Professor Mark Williams (an Anglican Priest) and Danny Penman.

In secular mindfulness the focus is on the breath or on the body. Some of the devotions suggest becoming aware of the breath or breathing deeply. Some too mention noticing senses or the body. As Christians we learn in the Bible that our bodies are 'fearfully and wonderfully made' (Psalms chapter 139 vv13-14) and that we are 'God breathed' (Genesis 2:7). Our first breath is a gift from God. Do check out the brilliant Nooma DVD by Rob Bell for a greater understanding.[2]

If you suffer from panic attacks, anxiety or have any condition which affects breathing, always consult your GP for advice in the first instance before undertaking meditation or breathing exercises.

---

[2] https://youtu.be/-EFLRDNAx-Y - accessed 31 Aug 22.

ONE
Scripture - Genesis 1:31 and 2:3

*God saw all that he had made, and it was very good.
Then God blessed the seventh day and made it holy,
because on it he rested from all the work of creation that
he had done.*

Reflection

Can you remember when you last felt really satisfied with something you had achieved, and then took time to sit back and enjoy it?

Life for many of us is lived at such a frantic pace, that no sooner do we finish one task than we start the next. We may even pride ourselves on our capacity to multitask!

In trying to do several things at once we don't give any of them the attention they require and deserve. The result is we bring what's called 'sub-optimal energy' to everything: we're not fully present to the task, or worse still, the person we may be with.

Today's words from the creation stories found in the opening chapters of the book of Genesis, tell us that even God took time to step back and enjoy what he had made. And he created the principle of Sabbath rest as a gift for us human beings made in his image, to do the same.

Mindful Thought

'What are the different ways you enjoy relaxing and resting? When your life gets too busy, these are the things that get squeezed out'[3]

---

[3] Liz Babbs, *Into God's presence* (Grand Rapids, Michigan USA: Zondervan, 2005) p 140.

Mindful Action

Try to just concentrate on completing one task. Don't answer the phone AND dash off an e-mail or clean your teeth WHILST cleaning down the sink. One moment. One task. See how it feels. Approaching tasks in this way means your thoughts aren't scattered and, though it may feel counterintuitive, you will actually be more productive. Factor in rest, or at least space to take a breath, between tasks.

Prayer

Think through me, thoughts of God;
My Father, quiet me,
Till in Thy holy presence, hushed
I think Thy thoughts with Thee.[4]

Your Space

[4] Amy Carmichael, *Gold Chord* (London: SPCK, 1932), quoted in Ruth Etchells, *Just as I am* (London: Triangle Books, SPCK, 1994) p32.

TWO
Scripture - Exodus 3:1-6

Now Moses was tending the flock of Jethro, his father-in-law, the priest of Midian, and he led the flock to the far side of the desert and came to Horeb, the mountain of God. There the angel of the Lord appeared to him in flames of fire from within a bush. Moses saw that though the bush was on fire it did not burn up.
So Moses thought, "I will go over and see this strange sight - why the bush does not burn up."
When the Lord saw that he had gone over to look, God called to him from within the bush, "Moses! Moses!"
And Moses said, "Here I am."
"Do not come any closer, "God said. "Take off your sandals, for the place where you are standing is holy ground." Then he said, "I am the God of your father, the God of Abraham, the God of Isaac and the God of Jacob."
At this, Moses hid his face,
because he was afraid to look at God.

Reflection

Bushes on fire in the parched and barren deserts of biblical Israel weren't an unusual sight. Had he been on 'autopilot' because he was doing what he did every day - looking after his father-in-law's sheep – Moses could so easily have missed the fact that, despite being aflame, the bush didn't burn up. It was that which led him to say, "I will go over and see this strange sight"

The Hebrew words that translate into this phrase, even more than the English, give a sense of stepping off a predetermined or familiar path, and that's what's so important in this encounter. I know that, at times, being so focused on 'what's next?' means I realise I can easily miss the 'burning bush' that's in front of me.

Brian Draper in his book *Soulfulness,* encourages us to be

"watchful with open-hearted presence."[5] That exactly describes Moses on this day and the experience proved to be life-changing for him and for others. If Moses hadn't gone to the bush, he would have missed the chance to encounter God, where he always is, in the present moment.

So, are you ready today to be interrupted? Are you ready to 'take off your shoes' in awe and wonder if God catches your attention through unexpected, or unusual ways?

Mindful Thought

"We know therefore that walking without shoes makes us notice our vulnerability and pay attention. We also associate barefoot walking with children and the intimacy of lovers. All this bears significance for the divine encounter."[6]

Mindful Action

At some point today (health permitting) remove your shoes or other footwear. Go outside so you can, like Moses, feel and experience the vulnerability of nothing separating you and the 'holy ground' beneath your feet.

Prayer

Come living God, when least expected,
when minds are dull and hearts are cold,
through sharpening word and warm affection
revealing truths as yet untold.

Come now, as once you came to Moses

---

[5] Brian Draper, *Soulfulness, Deepening the mindful life* (London, Hodder and Stoughton, 2016) p20.
[6] J. P. Williams, *Seeking the God Beyond, A Beginner's Guide to Christian Apophatic Spirituality* (London: SCM, 2018) p6.

within the bush alive with flame;
or to Elijah on the mountain,
by silence pressing home your claim. Amen.[7]

Your Space

---

[7] Alan Gaunt, *Come living God when least expected*, from Hymns Ancient and
Modern, 2013, (London, Hymns Ancient and Modern Ltd, 2013 edition) no 615.

THREE
Scripture - 1 Samuel 16:7

But the Lord said to Samuel, "Do not consider his appearance or height, for I have rejected him. The Lord does not look at the things people look at. People look at the outward appearance, but the Lord looks at the heart."

Reflection

Prejudice! What do you think of when you see that word? It quite literally means 'pre' 'judgement.' We all come to every situation with our pre-judgements. These are not based on fact but on factors - our race, gender, life experience, the culture we inhabit...

We live today in a very image-conscious culture. People are judged for the way they look or how wealthy or successful they are perceived to be. Today's verse shows that there's nothing new about this tendency. Here the prophet Samuel is seeking God's help in discerning who should succeed Saul as King of Israel. Saul had been tall and handsome, so Samuel was probably looking for the new and improved version from Jesse's sons. However, God warns Samuel against judging by outward appearance. Image and appearance don't reveal who people really are, or their true value. Learning to practise being mindful helps to address this very human inclination to make quick, sharp, often inaccurate judgments. It can also be the means of noticing things we might otherwise miss.

Learning to be non-judgemental doesn't prevent us from making any decisions. Rather it means that when we encounter thoughts and emotions arising, positive or negative, we recognise them for what they are - thoughts - take time to pause and, for Christians, listen to what God may be saying. And then, as Samuel did, hopefully make the decision with more wisdom and discernment; also recognising that only God can see 'the heart' and therefore only he can accurately judge people.

Mindful Thought

"Do not judge, or you too will be judged. For in the same way you judge others, you will be judged, and with the measure you use, it will be measured to you.
Why do you look at the speck of sawdust in your brother's eye and pay no attention to the plank in your own eye? How can you say to your brother, 'Let me take the speck out of your eye,' when all the time there is a plank in your own eye? You hypocrite, first take the plank out of your own eye, and then you will see clearly to remove the speck from your brother's eye."
(Matthew 7: 1-5).

Mindful Action

Recognise that as human beings we bring our 'pre-judgement' with us to every situation. Recognise the brain's tendency to react rather than respond. Give yourself a few moments and then ask, "what is the story I am telling myself?" Could you ask God to give you another story? Or could you reserve judgement until you have collected more information? Keep the verses from Matthew at the forefront of your mind. Choose to love not to judge.

Prayer

God be in my head, and in my understanding.
God be in my eyes, and in my looking.
God be in my mouth, and in my speaking.
God be in my heart, and in my thinking.
God be at my end, and at my departing.[8]

---

[8] From the Sarum Primer, quoted in David Adam, *The Rhythm of Life, Celtic Daily Prayer* (London SPCK, Triangle, 1996) p 83.

Your Space

FOUR
Scripture - Psalm 8:3-9

*When I consider your heavens, the work of your fingers,
the moon and the stars, which you have set in place,
what is man that you are mindful of him,
the son of man that you care for him?
You made him a little lower than the heavenly beings and
crowned him with glory and honour.
You made him ruler over the works of your hands;
you put everything under his feet:
all flocks and herds, and the beasts of the field,
the birds of the air, and the fish of the sea,
all that swim the paths of the seas.
O LORD, our Lord,
how majestic is your name in all the earth!*

Reflection

We simply had to include this scripture. This psalm of David is one of the most significant texts we refer to in our publication, *Mindfulness as Mission Gift* (Fresh Expressions, 2022).

As Christians we can only learn to be mindful in this present moment, if we realise that God was first mindful of us. David is filled with awe at the thought that the God who created everything also created and loved human beings (and bear in mind David's limited understanding of 'everything' when there was no such thing as the Hubble telescope). How much more in awe should we be today with our greater knowledge of the vastness of the universe? Do we journey through our day recognising the detail of all God has created? How mindful he was when creating us? How mindful of us he still is.

Mindful Thought

"Though our feelings come and go, God's love for us does not."[9]

Mindful Action

As you go about your day today utilise all of your senses to really notice creation - appreciate all the sights, sounds and smells and the fact that they are all gifts from God.

Prayer

Creator God, thank you for your mindfulness of us. Thank you that no matter what circumstances we find ourselves in today you already know. You go ahead of us, and your Spirit is within us. Help us to be mindful and thankful of that knowledge. Amen

Your Space

---

[9] C.S. Lewis, *Mere Christianity* (New York: Harper Collins, 2001) pp 132-133.

FIVE
Scripture - Psalm 34:4-5

I sought the Lord, and he answered me; he delivered me from all my fears. Those who look to Him are radiant; their faces are never covered with shame.

Reflection

Shame - Overcoming the hidden iceberg.
Guilt is what we feel when we've done something wrong. Shame is quite different. Shame is what we feel when we think (for whatever reason) that there is something fundamentally wrong, flawed, and unacceptable with the person we are. It colours all of our thinking and diminishes our perception of ourselves. It saps our energy and confidence such that we view ourselves with a strong negativity bias. It's possible to wallow in shame and accept the false message that shame seeks to impose on us.

Often shame comes calling if we have faced rejection or verbal abuse. Words of anger or malice can leave a residual trace of trauma in us which can be triggered again if we face similar circumstances. How can we escape this cycle?

Mindful Thought

Jesus died in your place to take away all your guilt and shame. It is finished. From the cross he said that it was. Focus now on your freedom in Him.

Mindful Exercise

"Those who look to Him are radiant; their faces are never covered with shame."

Take 10 minutes now.

Focus on your breathing.

Focus your spiritual gaze on the radiant face of Jesus Christ.

Breathing in and breathing out.

Let the radiance and warmth of his love melt away all shame from you like ice melting away in the heat of summer

Stand in your true identity as beloved of God.

Prayer

Lord Jesus, thank you for the radiance of your love that comes to me again and again to melt away all fear and shame. I trust in you and your love towards me, to free me from shame and enable me to walk in spiritual freedom. Amen.

Your Space

SIX
Scripture - Psalm 37:7

Be still before the Lord and wait patiently for him; do not fret when people succeed in their ways, when they carry out their wicked schemes.

Reflection

Psalm 37 is a song of great encouragement. It's written by an elderly man (see verse 25) who, with all the benefit of hindsight and with the advantage of a lifetime of experience to draw on, is reassured that even when things seemed to be falling apart, God has been mindful of him. He is convinced that ultimately good will triumph over evil, and there is therefore no need in the present moment to give in to anxiety and fear. Humanly this is difficult, particularly when the 'success' we see in others doesn't line up with Kingdom values. It's easy to be drawn into envy and, to use a 21st century term, 'FOMO' (fear of missing out) believing that to be busy or successful is the way of finding significance.

In the light of this man's experience and example and the encouragement he offers, can we, when we find ourselves in such a place, be still before the Lord and "wait patiently" for Him?

Mindful Thought

"O, beware, my Lord, of jealousy; It is the green-eyed monster which doth mock the meat it feeds on."[10]

---

[10] William Shakespeare, *Othello, Act 3, Scene 3, line 165-166.*

Mindful Action

Take some moments today to reflect on your life, be mindful of specific ways in which God has been faithful to you, especially when things were tough or challenging.

Prayer

Eternal God, the light of the minds that know you,
the joy of the hearts that love you
and the strength of the wills that serve you:
grant us so to know you that we may truly love you,
so, to love you that we may truly serve you,
whose service is perfect freedom,
through Jesus Christ our Lord. Amen.[11]

Your Space

[11] After Augustine of Hippo 430, taken from *Prayer for the Day on Tuesday*, https://d3hgrlg6yacptf.cloudfront.net/5f209069c4808/content/pages/documents/1583843436.pdf - accessed 5 Aug 2022.

SEVEN
Scripture - Psalm 37:8

Do not lose your temper - it only leads to harm.

Reflection

I (Karen) have to confess this one is in our collection for me. When I am 'triggered' I barely recognise myself in my reactions. I feel like a wild animal. Which is, in the moment, precisely what I am. My body's 'prehistoric' system is switched on to protect me from imminent danger and I become super (or perhaps sub) human! It's not pretty! For so many years I was trapped in a cycle of shame. I would lose my temper over something fairly trivial and then beat myself up for feeling less than God's best. I am very grateful for my learning on the vagus nerve and commend to you the writings of S.W. Porges and MGabor Maté for further reading.[12]

The practice of mindfulness and meditation tones the vagus nerve and takes the amygdalae in the brain out of hyper alert. This means we become more able to respond in the moment rather than react. Equally important is the practice of self-compassion which enables us to let go of self-judgement and recover more quickly if we have 'reacted.' That way we can apologise for our poor behaviour. However, we may still need to (re)establish whatever boundary we feel has been violated that triggered our anger in the first place. Anger is an emotion which, when rightly channelled, serves a purpose. We need to be mindful of that and treat it as a friend to be valued and respected.

---

[12] Porges, S. W., *The polyvagal theory: neurophysiological foundations of emotions, attachment, communication, and self-regulation.* (New York, W.W. Norton 2011) and how our bodies hold trauma Gabor, M., *When the body says no: the cost of hidden stress.* (Toronto: A.A. Knopf Canada 2003)

Mindful Thought

"Anger is a wind which blows out the lamp of the mind."[13]

"May God bless us with anger at injustice, oppression and exploitation of people so that we may work for justice, freedom and peace."[14]

Mindful Actions

Learn to recognise how you are 'triggered.'
Don't overfill your day and put yourself under stress.
Acknowledge your anger and, if necessary, express it appropriately.
Practice self-compassion if you do 'explode.'
Establish boundaries.

Prayer

Gracious God, give us righteous anger for the things that break your heart and a passion to make a difference in this world. Forgive us for those times when our reactions are inappropriate and give us grace to say we are sorry. Please prevent the enemy gaining a foothold through our words or actions. Amen

Your Space

---

[13] Robert Green Ingersoll Quotes from https://www.quotes.net/quote/14420 - accessed 4 Jul 2022.
[14] https://www.franciscans.ie/a-franciscan-blessing - accessed 4 Jul 2022.

EIGHT
Scripture - Psalm 45:1

My heart is stirred by a noble theme as I recite my verses for the king: my tongue is the pen of a skilful writer.

Reflection

The Psalm from which this verse is taken, is a poem to the king (possibly Solomon) on the occasion of his wedding. But the Psalm is also understood to be prophetic, pointing forward to Christ and his bride, the church, whose members in every generation are called to be stirred by his love and to praise him.

I'm especially struck though by the way in which the Psalm begins, with the twin ideas of 'reciting' and 'writing;' two ways of expressing such praise and gratitude.

Many people testify to the value of keeping a 'Gratitude Journal,' and the different ways in which this can prove to be beneficial. Developing the practice of routinely journaling our experiences and reflecting on them, can help improve our mental health and generally have a positive effect on our well-being.

And for the Christian, this isn't about being unhealthily self-focused, but rather can enable us to better trace the activity of God in our lives, restore perspective, and live more gratefully.

Mindful Thought

"The unexamined life is not worth living"[15], is a phrase attributed to Socrates. In terms of your current reflective

---

[15] https://www.cambridge.org/core/journals/think/article/abs/is-the-unexamined-life-worth-living-or-not/8D5EC7FCA494A8B9A5E5D02BADAB6182 - accessed 31 Aug 2022.

practice, how do these words encourage or challenge you?

Mindful Action

If this is something you don't already practice, at the end of today engage with a simple version of the 'Examen,' taking a few moments to reflect on, and maybe write down, three ways in which you have seen God at work today - and give him your thanks and praise.

Prayer

"My tongue will be the pen of a ready writer,
And what the Father gives to me I'll sing;
I only want to be his breath,
I only want to glorify the King."[16]

Your Space

---

[16] Ronnie Wilson, *I hear the sound of rustling*, from Mission Praise, (London: Collins, 1990), no 274.

NINE
Scripture - Psalm 46:10

"Be still and know that I am God…"

Reflection

How does that invitation land with you today?

Into an ancient time of chaotic conflict, God spoke these clarion words to the psalmist, "Be still and know that I am God." It was a powerful command to warring nations, but also an invitation (then and now) to every individual heart tired out and discouraged by the woes and battles around and within us.

Today, the news cycle brings us daily horror stories of suffering and injustice on an unprecedented scale. Public and private conversations are often polarised and enraged, and social media can mirror and magnify our worries and insecurities in ways our nervous systems understandably struggle to process peacefully. So, what can this invitation to "be still" mean for us, in the complexity and anxiety of our current age? An understanding of stillness as simply a lack of activity or motion is not as rich as the original Hebrew word. "Be still" comes from the Hebrew verb 'raphah' which means to let go, release your grasp, put down your weapons. And this word has a deeper root 'rapha' which means to cease from activity and be restored, replenished, sewn back together. So, carried in this simple English imperative "Be still" is actually a beautiful invitation to us from God to intentionally take some time to let go of whatever is causing us exhaustion, and rest in the loving presence of the Divine? Maybe it is in this practice of stillness that we can be replenished so that we may be all we can be in, and for the world? For me, these times of resting in stillness and silence with God mend my ragged soul when the world is too much and replenish me with peace and joy so I can be more fully and mindfully present to life as it is, not simply how I wish it to be. It is moving me from a life of anxiety to a life of trust, step by step.

Mindful Thought

"When I practice allowing myself to be seen and loved by the God who made me from dust, I start to carry an inner stillness with me back into the noise, like a secret. There is a quiet place inside me that I bring with me, and when I start to feel the questions, the fear, the chaos, I locate that quiet, that stillness, that grounded place."[17]

Mindful Action

Try taking just two minutes a day, somewhere quiet and without distractions, simply to be still. Feel the soles of your feet on the ground, and the rhythm of your breath.

Bring awareness to yourself, your surroundings, and the presence of God. Perhaps say to yourself, "Be still and know that I am God." Notice if there are thoughts and feelings that you are grasping or pushing away. No need to judge them but allow them to release as you soften your stance and rest in God's loving presence within and around you. If you feel distracted (which is totally normal!) just keep coming back to the verse or to the gentle rhythm of your breath. You could place a hand gently over your heart if that feels helpful, noticing the gift of your breath, the gift of life being brought to you by God, moment by moment.

---

[17] Shauna Niequist, *Present over Perfect (Grand Rapids, Michigan: Zondervan, 2016).*

Prayer

Loving God,

Thank you that you are always mindful of us, inviting us into communion with you. May we learn to rest and trust in your grace and presence, find strength in the deep stillness of those moments, and allow you to inspire and energise us for the life and work you have set before us.

Amen

Your Space

TEN
Scripture - Psalm 46:10

"Be still, and know that I am God! I will be honoured by every nation. I will be honoured throughout the world."[18]

Reflection

The essence of life is not what I do but who I am. "Be still and know that I am God" revolutionised my understanding of knowing God intimately. I had never focused on what the 'be' described. The 'be' is my life centred in the eternal now of God.

In reverence of the Holy One of Israel, I agree with the command to still my mind and know God in my heart. I worship the "I am" Moses encountered in the burning bush. I contemplate God is seeking me far more than I seek after him and that he desires for me to experience the awareness of his presence. I open my heart to receive and listen for his voice in the stillness.

I release my fears and confess my sins in my heart's secret chambers. My one desire and one thought are to know God. In the silence, I die to my will and ego and seek to convert my heart to God.

Mindful Thought

In the silence, I purposely seek to sit at the feet of Christ and let the cares of the world become still and silent within me.

Mindful Exercise

In a quiet prayer time, start by reciting, "Be still and know that I am God." As you repeat the verse, leave off a word or two each time as you pray through it and "be" who you are in His presence.

Be still and know that I am God
Be still and know that I am
Be still and know
Be still
Be

Prayer

Lord Jesus, thank you for loving me before I loved You. Please show me the ways that I am trying to find joy and fulfilment apart from You. Please calm my restless soul and help me be still. Allow me to know in the deepest parts of my being that I am loved by You, that who I am in You is what matters. Help me to be still and know that You are God. To be still and know that You are the I Am. To be still and know. To be still. To be. Amen.[19]

Your Space

---

[19] Bane, P & Litton, M., *In the Presence of Jesus. A 40-Day Guide to the Intimacy with God You've Always Wanted* (Illinois: Tyndale House Publishers, 2021)

ELEVEN
Scripture - Psalm 115:12

The Lord has been mindful of us, He will bless us.[20]

Reflection

In the NIV version of this scripture, it says "The Lord has remembered us." Along with 'mindful' there are a multitude of meanings to the word 'remember' such as, to bring to mind, or think of again. It also implies a keeping in memory that may be effortless or unwilled. God is mindful of us, remembers us, because God simply can't do anything else. The opposite of remembering is forgetting. It can feel really hurtful when somebody forgets us or forgets about us or forgets what we've told them. But it is the nature of God to be mindful and to remember and not to forget. There is no detail of our life which he forgets. And his remembering is not in order to remind us of our shortcomings or failings, as the world is wont to do. As it says in Psalm 103:12, "as far as the east is from the west, so far has he removed our transgressions from us." His desire is to bless us, as the rest of this Psalm makes clear.

We can rest in the amazing truth that God remembers us and cares for us. And, if we are truly mindful of this then we can perhaps practise recognising when our 'remembering' or 'not remembering' may not be helpful or kind. Maybe too we can accept our thoughts and allow any unhelpful 'remembering' to pass and seek to bless others as God blesses us.

Mindful Thoughts

"Before you speak, ask yourself if what you are going to

---

[20] Scripture taken from the *New King James Version*. Copyright © 1982, Used by permission of Thomas Nelson.

say is true, is kind, is necessary, is helpful. If the answer is no, maybe what you are about to say should be left unsaid."[21]

"...slow down and self-edit and ask yourself the three things you must always ask yourself before you say anything: "Does this need to be said?" "Does this need to be said by me?" "Does this need to be said by me now?" [22]

Mindful Action

Have in mind how God is mindful of/remembers us, in order to respond rather than react. Allow yourself a few (perhaps prayerful) moments and then filter your words through the above tests ...

Prayer

Thank you, Lord, that you are a God who remembers everything yet still chooses to bless us. Amen

Your Space

---

[21]Bernard Meltzer
https://www.brainyquote.com/quotes/bernard_meltzer_157511 - accessed 25 Aug 2022.
[22]Craig Ferguson
https://www.quotemaster.org/qa769ea28789eaf3e1b63ac8048ce7b4a - accessed 25 Aug 2022.

TWELVE
Scripture - Proverbs 4:5-6

Trust in the Lord with all your heart and lean not on your own understanding. In all your ways acknowledge him, and he will make your paths straight.

Reflection

These verses have been important to me (Chris) for many years, especially the imagery of 'leaning,' with its sense of being able to 'put your weight on something.' In this instance, having confidence that even if other people might let us down, God won't. He can be trusted.

More recently, it's the phrase 'in all your ways acknowledge him,' which stands out for me. Thank God we can cry out to him in times of crisis. But the invitation here is to acknowledge or invite him into every aspect of our lives; whether that's 'the good, the bad or the ugly'! As I know from experience, it's all too easy to compartmentalise and, when we do this, we miss out on God's healing and transforming work in and through us.

When we're ready to be open, vulnerable, and as present to God as we can possibly be, the promise is that 'he will make your paths straight.' This isn't of course some magic, spiritual formula, where nothing will ever go wrong again. But the more we're tuned into how mindful of, and concerned for, all his children God is, the more confident we will become in each moment and situation of his loving presence in our journey.

Mindful Thought

"Acceptance of God's will does not mean submission or resignation to 'whatever will be will be.' Rather, we actively wait for the Spirit to move and prompt, and then discern what to do next."[23]

Mindful Action

Take time to identify, and maybe write down, any areas of your life that may be currently 'closed off' from God. Then consciously make him a part of everything you are and do today.

Prayer

Merciful God, You understand all, forgive all, absorb and encompass all. Teach us not to dwell on the past, or be filled with fear for the future, but rather to live fully in the present, breathing in time with your divine breath and spirit. Amen.[24]

Your Space

[23] Henri J.M.Nouwen, with Michael J Christensen & Rebecca J. Laird, *Discernment: Reading the Signs of Daily Life* (HarperOne, 2013 by the estate of Henri J.M. Nouwen), p8.

[24] Ian Bradley, Prayer for the Day, Volume II, (London: Watkins, 2005), p 109.

THIRTEEN
Scripture - Isaiah 30:19-21.

People of Zion, who live in Jerusalem, you will weep no more. How gracious he will be when you cry for help! As soon as he hears, he will answer you. Although the Lord gives you the bread of adversity and the water of affliction, your teachers will be hidden no more; with your own eyes you will see them. Whether you turn to the right or to the left, your ears will hear a voice behind you saying, "This is the way; walk in it."

Reflection

Mindfulness is very much about being in touch with the senses. If we are mindful, then we are present to the presence of God. For people of faith, making decisions includes the added dimension, and sometimes infuriating complication, of trying to consider what God has to say on the matter. When we are flustered and anxious and overwhelmed it's harder to hear the voice of God. That makes it difficult to know what to do. All of us will have known those paralysing moments when an urgent decision is needed, but it's still not clear what to say, or which way to go, as different voices reverberate around our minds. When we are able to take that moment to "Be still and know that he is God" then our minds can become clear - our ears can be opened - our eyes no longer clouded over, and we can see the correct way forward in a situation.

Someone once said, "you can only steer a moving ship."[25] Rather than allowing the thoughts to proliferate there are times when we should just take the first steps and begin moving, trusting that things will become clearer as we progress. Remember the promise that "whether you turn to the right or to the left your ears will hear a voice behind

---

[25]https://leadershipvoices.com/2014/11/22/you-can-only-steer-a-moving-ship/ - accessed 2 Aug 2022.

you saying, "This is the way; walk in it."

Mindful Thought

"When faced with a decision, many people say they are waiting for God. But I understand in most cases, God is waiting for me."[26]

Mindful Action

If possible, take a walk today. Pause at a fork in the path or at a crossroads. Offer any decisions, or feelings of indecision, to God in prayer.

Prayer

Loving God, tune the ears of my heart to your promptings, and make me more ready to hear and respond to your voice, whether that be in comfort or correction, that I may know more clearly your guidance, this, and every day. I pray this in the name of Jesus Christ our Lord. Amen

Your Space

---

[26]Andy Andrews. https://www.goodreads.com/quotes/10491-when-faced-with-a-decision-many-people-say-they-are - accessed 4 Jul 2022.

FOURTEEN
Scripture - Lamentations 3:21-23

Yet this I call to mind and therefore I have hope.
Because of the Lord's great love we are not consumed,
for his compassions never fail. They are new every
morning; great is your faithfulness.

Reflection

It's an understandable reaction for many of us, to anticipate the future with a mix of longing and fear, especially when the present moment is tough. That was certainly the case for the people of the prophet Jeremiah's day. They'd come to the painful realisation that the reason their world had fallen apart, symbolised in the destruction of the holy city of Jerusalem, was in large measure due to their disobedience to God.

Into this seemingly hopeless situation come today's beautiful and hope-filled words, that sees Jeremiah looking away from himself and the mess around him toward God. Jeremiah chooses his thoughts consciously and deliberately. He "calls to mind" the unchanging love, faithfulness, and mercy of God, drawing on his prior knowledge and experience.

Thoughts come into our mind uninvited, but it is a choice whether we hook onto them or allow them to pass and to choose a different thought - a more positive one - as Jeremiah did. In doing this he knows he can find hope both for the present moment and for the future. And we can too. God's gifts of love and compassion are renewed each and every day, including today, for us!

Mindful Thought

"Great is thy faithfulness! Great is thy faithfulness!

Morning by morning new mercies I see;
all I have needed thy hand hath provided,
great is thy faithfulness, Lord, unto me."[27]

Mindful Action

Is there something in your life which you think God can't forgive? Reach out to him today. His unchanging love and mercy are greater than any sin, and he assures us of forgiveness. In Psalm 103 v12 we are reminded "as far as the east is from the west, so far has he removed our transgressions from us."

Trusting in God's faithfulness, moment by moment, gives us confidence to think differently about ourselves and of God which enables us to live differently.

Prayer

Compassionate God, thank you that your mercy, love, and goodness are gifts which are new every morning. I come humbly before you asking that you might grant forgiveness, healing and hope in my life and in the lives of those I love today. In the name of Christ our Lord. Amen.

Your Space

---

[27] Thomas O. Chisholm, *Great is thy faithfulness,* from Ancient and Modern (London: Hymns Ancient and Modern, 2013), no 680.

FIFTEEN
Scripture - Matthew 2:1-12

The Magi Visit the Messiah
After Jesus was born in Bethlehem in Judea, during the time of King Herod, Magi from the east came to Jerusalem and asked, "Where is the one who has been born king of the Jews? We saw his star when it rose and have come to worship him."

When King Herod heard this he was disturbed, and all Jerusalem with him. When he had called together all the people's chief priests and teachers of the law, he asked them where the Messiah was to be born. "In Bethlehem in Judea," they replied, "for this is what the prophet has written:

"'But you, Bethlehem, in the land of Judah,
are by no means least among the rulers of Judah;
for out of you will come a ruler
who will shepherd my people Israel.'"
Then Herod called the Magi secretly and found out from them the exact time the star had appeared. He sent them to Bethlehem and said, "Go and search carefully for the child. As soon as you find him, report to me, so that I too may go and worship him."

After they had heard the king, they went on their way, and the star they had seen when it rose went ahead of them until it stopped over the place where the child was. When they saw the star, they were overjoyed. On coming to the house, they saw the child with his mother Mary, and they bowed down and worshipped him. Then they opened their treasures and presented him with gifts of gold, frankincense and myrrh. And having been warned in a dream not to go back to Herod, they returned to their country by another route.

Reflection

The season during which the magi visited is referred to as 'epiphany.' An epiphany moment is a sudden realisation; which could be described as a waking up or even becoming mindful. There is so much that could be said about how mindful the magi were, not least in paying attention to the warning in their dreams, returning another way, not wishing harm to befall the new-born infant. But what is most striking in this passage is how caught up they were in the present moment. They follow the star - they know how to read the skies - and when it stops, they know that this is where the promised ruler would be born. Picture the scene. The warmth and the light and the joy are almost tangible. Nothing else matters to them at that moment than bowing down in worship and giving this baby boy the meaningful gifts, they have chosen. These were important men often referred to as Kings or Wise men, but they realise that they are not just in the presence of a baby but the saviour of the World,

Mindful Thought

"They wanted to see Jesus. Like the Shepherds they were not satisfied with the spectacular star they saw in the night sky. To be a witness of the blazing orb was a privilege, but for the magi it wasn't enough to see the light over Bethlehem; they wanted to see the Light of Bethlehem."[28]

Mindful Action

Light a candle and sit in front of it giving it your whole focus. As you look at the light, think about Jesus. Remain in the moment. If you find your mind wandering - which you will - just draw yourself back to the light and thoughts

---

[28] Max Lucado, *In the Manger* (Thomas Nelson publishing: Nashville, Tennessee 2012) p 81.

of Christ. Whenever you light a candle let this act as a reminder that Jesus is always present.

Prayer

Jesus, light of the World, we ask you to shine into the darkest places of our lives and fill them with your light. Help us, we pray, radiate your light in all we think and say and do, and build your Kingdom in and through us. Amen

Your Space

SIXTEEN
Scripture - Matthew 6:25-34

"Therefore I tell you, do not be anxious about your life, what you will eat or what you will drink, nor about your body, what you will put on. Is not life more than food, and the body more than clothing? Look at the birds of the air: they neither sow nor reap nor gather into barns, and yet your heavenly Father feeds them. Are you not of more value than they? And which of you by being anxious can add a single hour to his span of life? And why are you anxious about clothing? Consider the lilies of the field, how they grow: they neither toil nor spin, yet I tell you, even Solomon in all his glory was not arrayed like one of these. But if God so clothes the grass of the field, which today is alive and tomorrow is thrown into the oven, will he not much more clothe you, O you of little faith? Therefore do not be anxious, saying, 'What shall we eat?' or 'What shall we drink?' or 'What shall we wear?' For the Gentiles seek after all these things, and your heavenly Father knows that you need them all. But seek first the kingdom of God and his righteousness, and all these things will be added to you. Therefore do not be anxious about tomorrow, for tomorrow will be anxious for itself. Sufficient for the day is its own trouble.''[29]

Reflection

The above scripture defines mindfulness. Jesus is instructing the gathered crowds not to focus on what food they need to eat that day or what clothing they need to wear. Nor to worry about tomorrow but to be in the present moment and seek out the good and positive in God's creation. He invites the crowd to focus on the lilies of the field and to really observe and witness their beauty. Jesus also links being in the present moment as an antidote to

---

[29] The Holy Bible, English Standard Version. (ESV) Copyright © 2001, 2016. Used by permission of Crossway Bibles.

worry and anxiety - a fundamental beneficial effect of living mindfully. I invite you to reflect on these words of Jesus and to think about what they mean to you personally.

Mindful Thought

Be mindful of the words you use today. They can bring joy, or they can cause suffering, even if that is not your intention.

Mindful Action

Take a moment at the end of today to recall all the positive and pleasant experiences you had. Write them down on individual pieces of paper and store them in a clear jar. Then sit back and let gratitude wash over you reflecting on all the moments of joy your life holds.

Prayer

Dear Father God,

We thank you for the wonder of your creation. Help us to know that we can seek out beauty and experience moments of joy, wherever we might find ourselves and whatever our circumstances may be. The view from a window, a photo of loved ones, being on a walk in the countryside. Help us to also know that by radiating love and kindness to ourselves and others, we can be released from emotional pain and suffering. Dear Lord, help me to breathe in and align my spirit with all that is divine, so that I may truly live a righteous life of love and forgiveness.

Amen.

Your Space

SEVENTEEN
Scripture - Matthew 9:18-22

While he was saying this, a synagogue ruler came and knelt before him and said, "My daughter has just died. But come and put your hand on her and she will live." Jesus got up and went with him, and so did his disciples. Just then a woman who had been subject to bleeding for twelve years came up behind him and touched the edge of his cloak. She said to herself, "If I only touch his cloak, I will be healed."
Jesus turned and saw her. "Take heart, daughter," he said, "your faith has healed you." And the woman was healed at that moment.

Reflection

In this section of Matthew's Gospel, we come across a string of stories in which people with great need encounter Jesus. What they share in common is that, in different ways, they are all desperate. We see Jesus responding personally and specifically to them.

Desperation has a way of making us bolder; just as the unnamed woman was. Because of her bleeding she was judged 'unclean,' and her very presence would be thought to make the crowds around Jesus 'unclean.' She risked facing their wrath. And indeed, that of Jesus, a Jewish man.

From his immediate response, Jesus was clearly both in tune with his body as well as mindful of the deep needs of the woman in this moment. He responded immediately with immense love and compassion. This fits perfectly with Matthew's telling of what Jesus says in the Sermon on the Mount (5:3 NLT) "God blesses those who are poor and realize their need for him, for the Kingdom of Heaven is theirs."

There are a couple of things to note. Firstly, she is

unnamed which suggests it could have been anybody, that includes you and me. Also, the woman had struggled with her particular problem for at least twelve years. This speaks of the fact that no matter how deeply rooted or for how long we may have been troubled by something - physical, emotional, or relational - if we reach out, the presence and touch of Jesus can bring us healing and release.

Mindful Thought

"Touch tells (individuals) they are still of value whatever their physical or mental condition. So often touch speaks louder than words. It restores a sense of value. It conveys unquestioning acceptance. It facilitates a release of emotional feelings. It communicates where words fail. It expresses concern and compassion. We should never underestimate the fact that touch is the simplest and most healing form of human contact."[30]

Mindful Action

Feelings of isolation and desperation register in the part of our brain associated with emotional processing. Today, rather than trying to silence any such feelings, acknowledge and welcome them without any sense of self-condemnation or shame and then simply allow them to pass. It may help to write the feelings down.

From a practical perspective think about working with a professional therapist to work through the feelings and, if trauma is being held in the body, to find release.

---

[30] Bill Kirkpatrick, *Going Forth: A Practical and Spiritual Approach to Dying and Death* (London: Darton, Longman &Todd, 1997), p16.

Prayer

Gracious and compassionate God, I can't find words to express what is happening in my life at the moment; but I reach out to you in faith. I trust that, in Jesus' name, you will hear and respond to me and that I will feel your loving and healing touch. Amen.

Your Space

EIGHTEEN
Scripture- Matthew 11:28-30

"Are you tired? Worn out? Burned out on religion? Come to me. Get away with me and you'll recover your life. I'll show you how to take a real rest. Walk with me and work with me—watch how I do it. Learn the unforced rhythms of grace. I won't lay anything heavy or ill-fitting on you. Keep company with me and you'll learn to live freely and lightly."[31]

Reflection

Our lives seem to be on fast-forward, propelled from one thing to the next. We fill our days yet feel like we don't inhabit our own lives. Jesus invites us to recover our lives, to "learn the unforced rhythms of grace." What might that be like?

I want to linger with the words 'unforced,' 'rhythms' and 'grace.'

The word 'unforced' startles me a bit because I don't think of myself as a person who forces anything. But the truth is that I buy into the managerial, make-things-happen approach to life that dominates Western culture. To live 'unforced' would mean for me to pay more attention to the invitations arising beneath the surface of my busyness. 'Unforced' turns my gaze to the unfolding of life, with an eye to what God might be up to in this very moment. As I relax into unforced life, I become attentive, not passive.

'Rhythms' are different from schedules. Schedules tend to be rigidly enforced by the clock, driving us ever onward. Rhythms are more flow-oriented, reflecting organic patterns of life, an organising pulse, like our heartbeat or

---

[31] Scripture taken from *The Message.* Copyright © 1993, 1994, 1995, 1996, 2000, 2001, 2002, 2018. Used by permission of NavPress Publishing Group.

breathing. Rhythms require pauses, rests that deepen and fuel the overall pattern. What rhythms are already present in my life? How might I embrace them?

The word 'grace' is so familiar I can miss its powerful challenge! While the world values achievement and productivity, grace awakens me to the deeper truth that life is a sheer gift that I did not plan, produce, or achieve. The world is not an object to be acted upon, but a sacred, astonishing reality in which God invites me to participate. What helps me see the grace flowing at the heart of all things?

What calls to you in "unforced rhythms of grace?" What would you need to let go of in order to follow this path? Come! Walk the Jesus way! Live freely and lightly!

Mindful Thought

"God shows up disguised as our lives."[32]

"Tell me, what is it you plan to do
with your one wild and precious life?"[33]

Mindful Action

Pause throughout your day – perhaps set a timer. Take 3 slow, deep breaths, noticing the "unforced rhythms." Be mindful of this gift of breath, a grace we cannot earn, schedule, or produce. Shaun Lambert suggests you might want to listen to the track, *Every Breath is Grace* by Alana Levandoski.[34]

---

[32]Paula D'Arcy, quoted in Richard Rohr, *Everything Belongs: The Gift of Contemplative Prayer* (Crossroads, 2003).

[33] Mary Oliver (New and Selected Poems, Boston, MA: Beacon Press, 1992).

[34] https://youtu.be/Dko_dQJdhgc - accessed on 31 Dec 2022.

Prayer

Holy One, help me see your unforced rhythms of grace today.

Your Space

NINETEEN
Mark 1:35-37

Very early in the morning, while it was still dark, Jesus got up, left the house and went to a solitary place where he prayed. Simon and his companions went to look for him, and when they found him they exclaimed: "Everyone is looking for you!"

Reflection

I doubt whether Jesus ever woke up and thought "I wonder what I can find to do today!" The gospels make it clear that Jesus was a busy man. He was often under pressure from people's demands and expectations - just as we can be. However, he was committed to 'intentional withdrawal.' This enabled him to sustain the intense engagement and effectiveness that characterised his life and ministry. In making time alone seeking God a priority, the 'mindful Jesus' offers us a model for life through his example. Does your life emulate the rhythm exemplified in Christ? If so, will you be better prepared and equipped for both the opportunities, as well as the pressures, and demands that might come your way today?

Mindful Thought

"Spiritual identity means we are not what we do, or what people say about us. We are the beloved daughters and sons of God." [35]

Mindful Action

You may be a 'lark,' or an 'owl'! Whichever, resolve today

---

[35] Henri Nouwen, https://www.brainyquote.com/quotes/henri_nouwen_588373 - accessed on 7 Jun 2022.

to ensure that at some point in the day, you give yourself permission to have some 'solitary moments'.

Prayer

O what a gift, what a wonderful gift,
Who can tell the wonders of the Lord.
Let us open our eyes, our ears, and our hearts,
It is Christ the Lord, it is he. Amen.[36]

Your Space

---

[36] Chorus of the *Canticle of the Gift*,
https://www.godsongs.net/2017/04/canticle-of-the-gift-christ-our-lord-and-our-king.html - accessed on 31 May 2022.

TWENTY
Scripture - Mark 6:30-32

The apostles gathered around Jesus and reported to him all they had done and taught. Then, because so many people were coming and going that they did not even have a chance to eat, he said to them, "Come with me by yourselves to a quiet place and get some rest." So they went away by themselves in a boat to a solitary place.

Reflection

This invitation from Jesus, comes after the disciple's first, exciting but demanding, piece of evangelism. Mark tells us how God had been powerfully at work through them (Mark 6:22-23). Jesus didn't then say to them, "Get back out there and do some more kingdom work!" Instead, mindful of their well-being, and given the fact that the disciples had poured themselves out, Jesus acts counter-intuitively in telling them that they need to step aside from the busyness; exciting and fulfilling as it may be. The word here for 'rest' in the original Greek of the New Testament is 'anapauo,' which conveys rest in its totality, involving body, mind, and spirit.[37]

Mindful Thought

"Half an hour's meditation each day is essential, except when you are busy. Then a full hour is needed."[38]

---

[37] Adapted from *Mindfulness as Mission Gift,* Openshaw K. & Edmondson C. Fresh Expressions Publication 2022, p11.
[38] Saint Francis de Sales, quoted on
https://www.goodreads.com/quotes/8309078-half-an-hour-s-meditation-each-day-is-essential-except-when - accessed on 13 Jun 2022.

Mindful Action

Do you need to move from "Can I afford the time to step aside," to "I can't afford not to", for your own sake, that of your relationships, and so that your work is actually more effective? If not even having a chance to eat in your day resonates with you, intentionally find at least 10 to 15 mindful minutes, to draw breath, switch your phone or other devices off, and rest.

Prayer

Almighty God, you have made us for yourself
and our hearts are restless till they find their rest in you.
So lead us by your Spirit,
that in this life we may live to your glory,
and in the life to come, enjoy you forever. Amen.

Based on the words of St Augustine.[39]

Your Space

---

[39] https://d3hgrlq6yacptf.cloudfront.net/5f209069c4808/content/pages/documents/1583843436.pdf - accessed 16 Aug 22.

TWENTY-ONE
Scripture - Mark 8:33

But when He had turned around and looked at His disciples, He rebuked Peter, saying, "Get behind Me, Satan! For you are not mindful of the things of God, but the things of men."[40]

Reflection

Drop the Story.

Three times in the gospel of Mark Jesus prophesies that he will die on the cross and rise again. The first time Jesus says this, Peter rebukes him. Peter doesn't want Jesus to be the suffering Messiah but the triumphant Messiah. Jesus' reply is, "Get behind Me, Satan! For you are not mindful of the things of God, but of the things of men."

We can have two stories in our head. A human story in which we seek to anxiously save ourselves, avoiding pain and difficulty. Culture teaches us this. We avoid it automatically; we don't have to work at it. Our minds are always running 'simulations' that we believe are real. But Jesus tells us in this verse that we can have a new God-given story.

Through reflection on a piece of scripture like this one, we can begin to be mindful of the things of God, which might be to turn and face the difficulty.

One way we can deal with our automatic human stories of avoidance and anxious self-focus is to notice them and drop them. We can name it as a simulation rather than reality. This makes space for the God-story to come into our awareness.

---

[40] Scripture taken from the *New King James Version*. Copyright © 1982, Used by permission of Thomas Nelson.

What are the human stories jostling for your attention right now? What story dominates?

Mindful Thought

"Without intervention, we live our minds almost entirely in simulation mode...We need to be able to shift out of a simulation mode into a mindful one so that we can open our eyes and see what is actually around us vs. the virtual reality of our making."[41]

Mindful Action

Notice the stories you create today and practise dropping them, realising they are simulations rather than reality.

Meditate on a verse of scripture that encapsulates a value for you until that scripture begins to emerge into your awareness.

Prayer

May the love of Christ take hold of me
May the light of Christ shine in my heart
May I see the simulated stories I create
May I drop those stories
May I cultivate a God-given story that is a personal value of mine.
Amen.

---

[41] Dr Amishi Jha, *Peak Mind* (Piatkus, 2021) p201.

Your Space

TWENTY-TWO
Scripture Luke 1:46-55

Mary's Song (The Magnificat)

And Mary said:

"My soul glorifies the Lord
and my spirit rejoices in God my Saviour,
for he has been mindful
of the humble state of his servant.
From now on all generations will call me blessed,
for the Mighty One has done great things for me—
holy is his name.
His mercy extends to those who fear him,
from generation to generation.
He has performed mighty deeds with his arm;
he has scattered those who are proud
in their inmost thoughts.
He has brought down rulers from their thrones
but has lifted up the humble.
He has filled the hungry with good things
but has sent the rich away empty.
He has helped his servant Israel,
remembering to be merciful
to Abraham and his descendants forever,
just as he promised our ancestors."

Reflection

This is a wonderful example of God's mindfulness of Mary, a humble, teenage girl beneath notice in that society. It's also a great illustration of how his mindfulness evokes a mindful response from her.

The opening verse has a real 'mindful' feel to it. She is completely lost in praise and wonder at God; amazed that he has first of all noticed her and then done such wonderful things for her. Mary is so totally swept up in the moment that she sings. It's a whole person experience. Body, mind, and soul. It wells up and pours out of her. Imagine how you would have responded if the Angel Gabriel had brought you the news that you were to give birth to the saviour of the world.

Think of those things you do where you are completely 'in the moment' - your mind is no longer distracted. So often they are creative in nature. What are those things that you do when you might say "Gosh, where did the time go?"

Mindful Thought

"Music is the divine way to tell beautiful, poetic things to the heart."[42]

Mindful Action

Raise your voice in song today. Don't worry whether you have a good singing voice or not. There is a wealth of evidence to back the therapeutic power of song.

Prayer

Creator God, thank you for the gifts of voices to sing and ears to hear music. We pray for those who can't speak or hear. Thank you for Mary who, because she was mindful, was obedient to you and filled with joy at your mindfulness of her. Help us to be fully alive and alert to you, ourselves, and others in each and every moment. Amen

---

[42] Pablo Casals https://www.outofstress.com/music-heals-quotes/#1 - accessed 27 Jul 2022.

Your Space

TWENTY-THREE
Scripture - Luke 9:34-37

While he (Peter) was speaking, a cloud appeared and enveloped them, and they were afraid as they entered the cloud. A voice came from the cloud saying, "This is my Son, whom I have chosen; listen to him."
When the voice had spoken, they found that Jesus was alone. The disciples kept this to themselves, and told no-one at the time what they had seen.

Reflection

To be mindful is to be fully aware in the moment, without judgement or expectations. Mindful listening is key to experiencing such awareness and attentiveness.

Today's reading forms part of the experience known as the transfiguration of Jesus. He took Peter, James, and John to the top of a mountain to show them who he truly was, preparing them for the next stage of their journey together. They saw him in conversation with Moses and Elijah and in all the overwhelming nature of the experience Peter wasn't able to be fully present, leading him to suggest building three shelters for Jesus, Moses, and Elijah in order to prolong the moment!

God says, 'This is my Son whom I have chosen.' The most appropriate response for the disciples who were there, and for us today, is to be present, fully aware, and attentive to Jesus - to 'listen to him' without being distracted.

Mindful Thought

Our English word for 'obedience' is derived from two Latin words, 'ob' and 'audire,' which mean to listen keenly. In the monastic Holy Rule of St Benedict, the opening word is very simply 'Listen.' He goes on to say, "Listen carefully, my son, to the master's instructions, and attend to them with the ear of your heart."[43]

Mindful Action

In whatever situations you may find yourself today, commit to listening attentively for the 'sounds of God.' They may come through words of Scripture, through people, perhaps in nature or even in silence. Remember God speaks "at many times and in various ways." (Hebrews 1: 1)

Prayer

For our prayer today the invitation is to echo the simple but profound words of the young boy Samuel, "Speak, Lord, for your servant is listening." (1 Samuel 3:9)

Your Space

---

[43] Quoted in *Leaders Learning to Listen*, Chris Edmondson (DLT: London, 2010) p43.

TWENTY-FOUR
Scripture - Luke 13:10-13

On a Sabbath Jesus was teaching in one of the synagogues, and a woman was there who had been crippled by a spirit for eighteen years. She was bent over and could not straighten up at all. When Jesus saw her, he called her forward and said to her, "Woman, you are set free from your infirmity." Then he put his hands on her, and immediately she straightened up and praised God.

Reflection

Being attentive is one of the most powerful forces in the world. Many of the stories from the gospels are not about Jesus' encounters with the crowds, but his paying attention to an individual. The woman in this story is never named. She has lived with a severe disability for eighteen years but that didn't stop her coming to worship. We're not sure exactly at what point in the visiting rabbi's message it happened, but the Bible records three powerful words: "Jesus saw her." She walked out of the service that day healed and standing straight. This was all as a result of Jesus paying attention to her. Are there ways in which you could increase the 'paying attention' aspect of your life, to God as well as to others?

Mindful Thought

"Stand up straight and realise who you are, that you tower above your circumstances. You are a child of God. Stand up straight."[44]

---

[44]Maya Angelou. https://www.goodreads.com/quotes/3591554-stand-up-straight-and-realize-who-you-are-that-you - accessed 28 Aug 22.

Mindful Action

Most of Jesus' life-changing encounters were unplanned, so be prepared for any divine interruptions God may send your way. Pay attention. Look each person in the eye when they're speaking. Listen carefully and ask questions that communicate care and interest.

Prayer

Gracious God, may I live attentively today, listening to you speaking in many and varied ways: through Scripture, whispers of your Spirit, circumstances, nature, creation, and the people in our lives. Amen.

Your Space

TWENTY-FIVE
Scripture - Luke 15:11-21

The Parable of the Lost Son

Jesus continued: "There was a man who had two sons. The younger one said to his father, 'Father, give me my share of the estate.' So he divided his property between them.

"Not long after that, the younger son got together all he had, set off for a distant country and there squandered his wealth in wild living. After he had spent everything, there was a severe famine in that whole country, and he began to be in need. So he went and hired himself out to a citizen of that country, who sent him to his fields to feed pigs. He longed to fill his stomach with the pods that the pigs were eating, but no one gave him anything.

"When he came to his senses, he said, 'How many of my father's hired servants have food to spare, and here I am starving to death! I will set out and go back to my father and say to him: Father, I have sinned against heaven and against you. I am no longer worthy to be called your son; make me like one of your hired servants.' So he got up and went to his father. But while he was still a long way off, his father saw him and was filled with compassion for him; he ran to his son, threw his arms around him and kissed him."

Reflection

The younger son was definitely not mindful! He was living in the future. He asked for his share of the inheritance. An inheritance that should not have been bestowed until the death of his father. He lived mindlessly and "squandered his wealth."

The scripture says "When he came to his senses ..." this

was his moment of becoming mindful. In mindfulness, meditation is focused either on the breath or on the body. In the NRSV version of this passage the translation is "he came to himself." He had been 'out of his mind' and now had returned to it.

His father had clearly been sitting and waiting for his son. Shunning social etiquette he ran to his son, completely in the moment, and "filled with compassion ... threw his arms around him and kissed him."

It's a beautiful story of human love and forgiveness - it's an even more precious analogy of the love of God for each and every one of us, his children. No matter how far away we go or how badly we have behaved, his love for us is unconditional, he awaits our return with his arms flung wide.

Mindful Thought

"Many of my daily preoccupations suggest that I belong more to the world than to God. A little criticism makes me angry, and a little rejection makes me depressed. A little praise raises my spirits, and a little success excites me. It takes very little to raise me up or thrust me down. Often, I am like a small boat on the ocean, completely at the mercy of its waves. All the time and energy I spend in keeping some kind of balance and preventing myself from being tipped over and drowning shows that my life is mostly a struggle for survival: not a holy struggle, but an anxious struggle resulting from the mistaken idea that it is the world that defines me."[45]

Mindful Action

---

[45] Henri J.M. Nouwen, *Return of the Prodigal Son*
https://www.goodreads.com/work/quotes/169164-the-return-of-the-prodigal-son-a-story-of-homecoming - accessed 12 Sep 2022.

Our identity lies in being children of God. That is what defines us. Meditation and the practice of mindfulness can help with feelings of being 'cast about.' Can you recognise that what you are doing is thinking - your thoughts are proliferating - and take them captive, offering them in prayer and returning your mind to Christ. It can be helpful to use as a focus the words, taken from Luke 18:13 of the Jesus Prayer "Lord Jesus Christ, Son of God, have mercy on me (a sinner)."[46]

Prayer

Father of all,
We give you thanks and praise,
that when we were still far off
you met us in your Son and brought us home.
Dying and living, he declared your love,
gave us grace and opened the gate of glory.
Amen[47]

Your Space

---

[46] https://www.britannica.com/topic/Hesychasm - accessed 12 Sep 2022.
[47] Taken from the 'Prayer after Communion', in *Common Worship* (London: Church House Publishing) p182.

TWENTY-SIX
Scripture - John 1:35-39

The next day John was there again with two of his disciples. When he saw him passing by, he said, "Look, the Lamb of God!."
When the two disciples heard him saying this, they followed Jesus. Turning around, Jesus saw them following and asked, "What do you want?"
They said, "Rabbi, where are you staying?"
"Come," he replied, "and you will see."

Reflection

'What do you want?' Or perhaps more literally "'what do you seek?," are the first words of Jesus recorded in John's Gospel; so, there's no doubt his choice of words is significant. On one level, it sounds like a straightforward and practical question from a man who is being followed by two strangers, but in the mouth of Jesus, it's both more open-ended and penetrating.

It's a question that Andrew and his companion aren't sure how to answer, so, perhaps a bit lost for words, they respond with a question of their own "Where are you staying?" At this point, all they are seeking is more time to be with this man who has been cryptically described as 'the Lamb of God.' There could have been many moments in this brief encounter which might have meant things went differently. Andrew and his companion could have remained with John, who was their Rabbi. Jesus might not have been mindful that they were following him. He may not have invited them to come and follow. He did. Having stayed with Jesus, and seen, Andrew comes to realise he has found more than just another Rabbi. What do you want? What do you seek?

Mindful Thought

Picture Jesus asking you today "what do you want?" How will you respond? Do you know? You may, like Andrew, believe you have "found the Messiah" (v 41). What does that mean for your journey? What do you need to see?

Mindful Action

Be intentional and mindful in seeking and looking for signs of the presence of Christ in every place, person, and situation in which you find yourself today.

Prayer

Help us Lord to seek your face when we are not sure what it is we want. You have the words of eternal life, and we believe and know that you are the Holy one of God. Keep us ever mindful of that as we journey. Amen.

Your Space

TWENTY-SEVEN
John 3:16

For God so loved the world that he gave his only Son, so that everyone who believes in him may not perish but may have eternal life.[48]

Reflection

When we read this iconic verse, we tend to hear that God loved all of humanity, which makes sense as the verse continues to say that each person who believes will not perish. Originally written in Greek, the word we translate as 'world' is 'kosmos.' This can mean humanity but usually means the whole created order. Another Greek word, 'anthropos,' is more commonly used to signify humanity as separate to the rest of creation. If we read this verse as God so loved the whole of creation, we gain a different feel for the saving power of God. God will not abandon us as people, nor will God abandon the divine creation which is described as 'good' in Genesis, and we are commanded to be stewards of.

Mindful Thought

God's vision for creation is all encompassing and we, God's people, are interdependent on that creation.

Mindful Exercise

If you are able to go outside, find something to look at from nature using a gentle gaze, for example: a river flowing, animals in a field, a leaf, a flower, a tree etc. If you are

---

[48] The Holy Bible, New Revised Standard Version Bible: Anglicised Edition. Copyright © 1989, 1995. Used by permission of the Division of Christian Education of the National Council of the Churches of Christ in the United States of America.

unable to go outside, then find a picture of something from nature.[49]

Spend time looking at this part of the created world. Notice the light and shadows, the textures, the colours, the shape, the movement.

Notice your feelings as you look – do not judge these feelings simply pay attention to them.

As you continue to gaze, ask yourself how God may be calling you to protect and help the part of nature you are gazing at to thrive. How is God calling you to be part of the divine all-encompassing vision of salvation?

---

[49] Photograph used with permission of Stephen Radley, the contributor of this devotion. https://www.soulfulvision.uk

Prayer

Lord God, help me to see your face in all of creation this day and show me how to be a good steward of the beautiful world you entrusted me to live in. Amen

Your Space

TWENTY-EIGHT
Scripture John 12:1-3

Six days before the Passover, Jesus came to Bethany, where Lazarus lived, whom Jesus had raised from the dead. Here a dinner was given in Jesus' honour. Martha served, while Lazarus was among those reclining at the table with him. Then Mary took about a pint of pure nard, an expensive perfume; she poured it on Jesus' feet and wiped his feet with her hair. And the house was filled with the fragrance of the perfume.

Reflection

Do you have a favourite fragrance? I (Karen) have to say I love perfume. It's my "guilty pleasure." One of my favourite brands is called Creed. I've never had a bottle though. It is prohibitively expensive. I always pop some on when I visit luxury department stores or the duty free and really savour it. It doesn't say it in this reading from John but in the reading from Mark (14:4) we are told the perfume with which Mary anointed Jesus's feet cost a year's salary. Imagine that. If you think about it, you can almost smell it.

The senses are incredibly important in mindfulness. They help to anchor you in the moment. One way to help stop a sense of being overwhelmed is to notice what you can smell, what you can hear, what you can see. This scene is a particularly mindful one - all of the family are completely "in the moment." Martha is serving (and there is no hint of the distraction she displayed on another occasion) Lazarus is reclining at the table eating and drinking with his Master and his friend - the man who restored him to life. And Mary ... she wipes away the perfume with her hair. Such extravagant love. Jesus was honoured indeed.

Mindful Thought

"I hope readers will consider, especially in this age of the World Wide Web, that as miraculous as it is, we still need to be in the same room with all five senses if we are to empathize with each other."[50]

Mindful Action

Use all the senses at your disposal in your interactions with people today. Make eye contact. Listen well. Use touch, appropriately, to convey empathy. Be truly present to the other.

Prayer

Loving Lord, in our interactions with all those we encounter today,
give us we pray the overwhelming love and generosity of Mary, the focus and attention of Lazarus, and Martha's desire to serve others
Amen

Your Space

---

[50] Gloria Steinem
https://www.huffpost.com/entry/gloria-steinem-interview_b_9079758 - accessed 25 Jul 22.

TWENTY-NINE
Scripture - John 14:27

"Peace I leave with you; my peace I give you. I do not give to you as the world gives. Do not let your hearts be troubled and do not be afraid."

Reflection

Peace is a mindful choice. In some Bible versions the word 'give' can be translated as 'bequeath' that means it's an inheritance. Jesus is passing on the gift of being at peace. This verse does not suggest that nothing bad will happen; it is a reminder from Jesus that, ultimately, there is no need to be afraid or worried. Humanly the situation may feel overwhelming, but we need to be mindful that God, the Holy Spirit, IS in us and with us. The Christian mystic Mother Julian of Norwich famously said, "All shall be well and all manner of things shall be well."[51] We discovered a beautiful poem called "All shall be well" by Ann Lewin, which beautifully articulates the kind of peace referred to by John in this verse. We commend it to you. She talks about how Mother Julian must have said "All shall be well" sometimes through gritted teeth yet trusted that God was with her and found her peace in knowing that. We must too.

Mindful Thought

"God does not give us everything we want, but He does fulfil His promises, leading us along the best and straightest paths to Himself."[52]

---

[51] https://christianhistoryinstitute.org/incontext/article/julian/ - accessed 3 Sep 2022.
[52] Dietrich Bonhoeffer https://www.goodreads.com/quotes/1262068-god-does-not-give-us -everything-we-want-but-he - accessed 16 Sep 2022.

Mindful Action

Take a moment to breathe. Breathe longer on the outbreath than on the inbreath.[53] Practising this has physiological benefits and creates a feeling of peace and calm - from a Christian perspective perhaps you could pray whilst you do this. Breathe out anxiety. Breathe in the peace of God.

Prayer

Thank you, God, that you gave those words to your faithful servant, Lady Julian of Norwich, and that they have endured to inspire and comfort so many. Help us to breathe in the power of your spirit as you fill our minds, hearts, and bodies with the peace that only you can give and the knowledge that "all shall be well." Amen

Your Space

---

[53] https://www.psychologytoday.com/gb/blog/the-athletes-way/201905/longer-exhalations-are-easy-way-hack-your-vagus-nerve - accessed 3 Sep 2022.

THIRTY
Scripture - John 19:25-27

Near the cross of Jesus stood his mother, his mother's sister, Mary the wife of Clopas, and Mary Magdalene. When Jesus saw his mother there, and the disciple whom he loved standing nearby, he said to his mother, "Dear woman, here is your son," and to the disciple, "Here is your mother." From that time on, this disciple took her into his own home.

Reflection

Although learning to be mindful is very much about paying attention to whatever our personal experience is in the present moment, most of us each day also interact in various ways with other people. This means that our learning to be more mindful should affect how we relate to them. So, what might this look like? Whatever else, it surely includes a kind, compassionate and gentle awareness of the needs of others.

In the words of Jesus from today's verses, we are given the most extraordinary example of this being put into practice. They are spoken as he hung on the cross, with the salvation of the world in the balance. He is in the most excruciating physical, emotional and spiritual pain; he could have had every reason for not thinking about the feelings and fears of others. Yet, mindful of the needs of his dear mother and close friend John, somehow Jesus is enabled to 'see' (the word used in the text), beyond his own desperate situation, and make provision into the future, for their needs.

Mindful Thought

"Every person is Christ for me, and since there is only one Jesus, that person is the one person in the world at that moment."[54]

Mindful Action

Sit quietly and wait for somebody to emerge into your thinking. Could it be the prompting of the Holy Spirit to reach out? It may be that their present circumstances are painful or challenging. Regardless of whether that is the case or not God has put them on your heart. Take a few moments to breathe in an awareness of them. Breathe out and pray for them. If possible, make contact with them to see if there is any way, as Ronald Rolheiser says in his book *The Holy Longing*, you can be 'God with skin on'* for them today.[55]

Prayer

Thank you, Jesus, for the mystery of your broken heart, a heart broken by us and for us, that has become now the source of forgiveness and new life. The blood and water flowing from your side show me the new life that is given to me through your death. It is a life of intimate communion with you and your Father. But it is also a life that calls me to give all that I am in the service of your love for the world. Amen.[56]

---

[54] Mother Teresa, quoted in John Pritchard, *Living faithfully* (London, SPCK, 2013) p108.
[55] https://www.christiantoday.com/article/god-with-skin-on-learning-to-live-as-the-body-of-christ/131062.htm - accessed 31 Oct 2022.
[56] Henri J.M. Nouwen, *Heart speaks to heart: Three Gospel Meditations on Jesus* (Ave Maria Press, Indiana, 1989), p43.

Your Space

THIRTY-ONE
Scripture - John 20:11-16

Now Mary stood outside the tomb crying. As she wept, she bent over to look into the tomb and saw two angels in white, seated where Jesus' body had been, one at the head and the other at the foot.
They asked her, "Woman, why are you crying?"
"They have taken my Lord away," she said, "and I don't know where they have put him." At this, she turned around and saw Jesus standing there, but she did not realize that it was Jesus.
He asked her, "Woman, why are you crying? Who is it you are looking for?"
Thinking he was the gardener, she said, "Sir, if you have carried him away, tell me where you have put him, and I will get him."
Jesus said to her, "Mary."
She turned toward him and cried out in Aramaic, "Rabboni!" (Which means "Teacher").

Reflection

Grief! It's hideous, isn't it? Anyone who's experienced it, and most of us have, know the feeling. It's no wonder people speak of being "out of our mind" with grief. We become mindless, not mindful.

And this was no ordinary death. It was an untimely, barbaric, traumatic death. She stood and watched it happen…
Hardly surprising then that she didn't know Jesus when he called her name.

Grief, understandably, makes us irrational. She can't think straight. It must have felt like she was going crazy. This man, whom she loved, was first crucified and now … gone - from the tomb and from her life. How, where why? And who were these strange, unearthly creatures?

Was it the grief that meant she couldn't recognise Jesus? Did he now, in resurrection, look somehow different?

And then, he says her name "Mary." Turning towards him she was back in the present moment. And he's here. How must she have felt? How would you have felt? What would you say to Him?

Mindful Thought

"When I think of death, and of late the idea has come with alarming frequency, I seem at peace with the idea that a day will dawn when I will no longer be among those living ..."[57]

These words are from a poignant passage from *'When I think of Death'* Maya Angelou. Do read it in its entirety.

Mindful Action

Perhaps today you could sit quietly for a while gazing at a photograph of somebody you have loved and have now lost. Remind yourself of the promise that we will one day be reunited. Pray for that person, for yourself and for your loss.

Prayer

Comforter God,

Thank you for your promise that you came to bind up the broken-hearted. Heal the wounds of those who grieve today we pray.

Amen

---

[57] https://whatsyourgrief.com/wp-content/uploads/2015/02/maya-angelou.jpg - accessed 25 Jul 2022.

Your Space

THIRTY-TWO

Scripture - Acts 17:16-28

While Paul was waiting for them in Athens, he was greatly distressed to see that the city was full of idols. So he reasoned in the synagogue with both Jews and God-fearing Greeks, as well as in the marketplace day by day with those who happened to be there. A group of Epicurean and Stoic philosophers began to debate with him. Some of them asked, "What is this babbler trying to say?" Others remarked, "He seems to be advocating foreign gods." They said this because Paul was preaching the good news about Jesus and the resurrection. Then they took him and brought him to a meeting of the Areopagus, where they said to him, "May we know what this new teaching is that you are presenting? You are bringing some strange ideas to our ears, and we would like to know what they mean." (All the Athenians and the foreigners who lived there spent their time doing nothing but talking about and listening to the latest ideas.)

Paul then stood up in the meeting of the Areopagus and said: "People of Athens! I see that in every way you are very religious. For as I walked around and looked carefully at your objects of worship, I even found an altar with this inscription: to an unknown god. So you are ignorant of the very thing you worship—and this is what I am going to proclaim to you.

"The God who made the world and everything in it is the Lord of heaven and earth and does not live in temples built by human hands. And he is not served by human hands, as if he needed anything. Rather, he himself gives everyone life and breath and everything else. From one man he made all the nations, that they should inhabit the whole earth; and he marked out their appointed times in history and the boundaries of their lands. God did this so that they would seek him and perhaps reach out for him and find him, though he is not far from any one of us 'For in him we live and move and have our being.' As some of

84

your own poets have said, 'We are his offspring.'

Reflection

This, for me (Karen) is the passage of scripture I quote to Christians, often clergy, who are suspicious of the word 'mindfulness.' I've been asked if I could use another word. My reply is an emphatic 'no.' These were the verses which acted as a prompt to write MAMG. In this passage, the apostle Paul meets the people of Athens where they are, in their space, even quoting from their own poets. He recognises their religiosity - what we might now refer to as 'spiritual seeking' - and then seeks to share with them the 'unknown God' whom they are worshipping. He does this with "gentleness and respect" (1 Peter 3:15). If we hope to engage with people in the 21st century, then we must speak to them in a language they understand. 'Mindfulness' has become a bit of a buzzword - most people have heard of it. For me, my encounter with it has been personally transformational, and recognising the mindfulness of God and Jesus referred to in the Bible and the long, rich heritage of Christian tradition steeped in being mindful of the presence of God is a gift to share.

I want to close by repeating verse 28, "'For in him we live and move and have our being.' As some of your own poets have said, 'We are his offspring.'" God is with us - or perhaps I should say - we are with God in this present moment, we are his children. Let's be mindful of this.

Mindful Thought

"It is not only the proclamation of the whole truth that is needed today; it is the release of the spiritual reality which the truth expresses, and that can only be realised as we allow ourselves to be caught in the mighty on-flowing tide of the Spirit."[58]

Mindful Action

It's really easy when we are very familiar with something to speak in ways that aren't accessible to others. If you are a Christian, try not to slip into using jargon when speaking to others. Don't assume knowledge - not even when speaking to other Christians. Meet people where they are, and you may get the opportunity to proclaim the unknown God people don't realise they are worshipping.

Prayer

Father God,

You made the world and everything in it. Let everything in me praise your name. Help me to share the good news of Jesus with gentleness and respect and in ways that people can truly understand, so that they might love you as I do.

Amen.

Your Space

---

[58] Watchman Nee https://www.azquotes.com/quote/1122903?ref=proclamation - accessed 10 Oct 2022.

THIRTY-THREE
Scripture - Romans 12:1-2

Therefore, I urge you, brothers and sisters, in view of God's mercy, to offer your bodies as living sacrifices, holy and pleasing to God - this is your spiritual act of worship. Do not conform any longer to the pattern of this world, but be transformed by the renewing of your mind. Then you will be able to test and approve what God's will is - his good, pleasing and perfect will.

Reflection

In the first eleven chapters of Paul's letter to the Romans he speaks of the 'who,' 'why' and 'what' of being a Christian. Chapter 12 takes a new tack - he moves to the 'how' of finding and doing God's will. These verses act as a hinge moment.

The word 'sacrifices' here has echoes of the sacrificial system we read about in the Hebrew Scriptures. But, by contrast with offering a dead animal on the altar, Paul says being committed to doing God's will means offering the entirety of ourselves and our living to God. He longs for us to live as people with transformed minds, which doesn't just refer to our intellects, but the whole of our beings. Not easy! We are human so even our best efforts to do this will sometimes have mixed motives and messy outcomes. Paying attention to what our bodies - our 'gut' - the indwelling Spirit says, enables us to live differently.

A renewed commitment to be mindful of, and committed to, doing God's will sets us free to be a 'work in progress,' confident that God's purposes can be worked out, in us and through us, as we offer him our flawed best.

Mindful Thought

"Instead of playing religious roulette with formulas and master plans, perhaps we should first ask if being in God's will is a Christian's destination, or a way of travelling?"[59]

Mindful Action

In mindfulness the meditation is often on the body. In life we often act 'mindlessly' without an awareness of what our bodies may be telling us. Take time today to recognise your bodily responses to situations - your breathing deepening, your heart beating faster, your stomach churning. What might God be saying to you about his will? How do you need to respond in this moment in order not to conform to the pattern of the world?

Prayer

Lord renew my mind, as your will unfolds in my life,
In living every day in the power of your love.
Hold me close, let your love surround me.
Bring me near, draw me to your side.
And as I wait, I'll rise up like an eagle,
And I will soar with you
In living every day in the power of your love.[60]

---

[59] Fritz Ridenour, *How to be a Christian without being Religious* (California G/L Publications, 1974) p.90.
[60] Lyrics from the song by Geoff Bullock, *The power of your love* (Hillsong Worship, Universal Publishing Group, 1992.

Your Space

THIRTY-FOUR
Scripture - 1 Corinthians 2:14-16

The person without the Spirit does not accept the things that come from the Spirit of God but considers them foolishness, and cannot understand them because they are discerned only through the Spirit. The person with the Spirit makes judgements about all things, but such a person is not subject to merely human judgements, for "Who has known the mind of the Lord so as to instruct him?" But we have the mind of Christ.

Reflection

In these verses from 1 Corinthians Paul is explaining the ministry of the Holy Spirit. The Holy Spirit reveals Christ to us as the wisdom of God. Paul reminds us that all Christians have access to the "mind of Christ," but also warns us that we can easily allow ourselves to revert to being shaped by other influences within and around us. It is amazing that, as human beings, through the Holy Spirit we have the gift of the "mind of Christ," but discernment is required to ensure our actions align with the Holy Spirit and not the 'foolishness' of the world.

Mindful Thought

"One whose soul is thus awakened [to the indwelling of the Holy Spirit], actually has 'the mind of Christ'."[61]

Mindful Action

You may remember the 'WWJD' (What Would Jesus Do) wristbands. In any decisions that you have to make today

---

[61] Quote taken from Richard Rohr, Center for Action and Contemplation https://cac.org/daily-meditations/the-immensity-within-2022-06-07/ with author addition in square brackets.

ask yourself, 'What would Jesus think, say and do here?'
Begin to make this a regular practice in your life.

Prayer

May the mind of Christ my Saviour
Live in me from day to day.
By his love and power controlling
All I do and say.[62]

Your Space

---

[62] The first verse of *May the mind of Christ my Saviour,* lyrics by Katie Wilkinson (1859-1928. Ancient and Modern (London: Hymns Ancient and Modern Ltd, 2013), number 727.

THIRTY-FIVE
Scripture - 2 Corinthians 10:3-5

For though we live in the world, we do not wage war as the world does. The weapons we fight with are not the weapons of the world. On the contrary, they have divine power to demolish strongholds. We demolish arguments and every pretension that sets itself up against the knowledge of God, and we take captive every thought to make it obedient to Christ.

Reflection

In many ways the final verse of this scripture encapsulates the difference between 'secular' mindfulness and Christian mindfulness. There are many strategies to utilise in order to prevent what's known as 'thought proliferation' but, to continue St Paul's analogy of war, the Christian has an extra weapon in their armoury. We are not alone. In mindfulness the suggestion is to notice that what we are doing is 'thinking' and to recognise that, accept it and then allow thoughts to pass. There is one further step in Christian mindfulness - to 'capture the thought and make it obedient to Christ.' We are not alone with the thought or cast about. We need not allow the thought simply to pass, we give it to God - in prayer. We don't need to act on the thought, instead we can look to the life modelled by Jesus to show us what our next step should be.

Mindful Thought

"Trust in the LORD with all your heart and lean not on your own understanding; in all your ways submit to him, and he will make your paths straight."
Proverbs 3:5-6

Mindful Action

Today, if you find yourself too much 'in your own head' with thoughts swirling around, take a moment to recognise that you are thinking and that thoughts are just thoughts. Make a conscious decision to give those thoughts to God in prayer; either by praying aloud or perhaps by writing your thoughts down. Place them, either metaphorically or literally, at the foot of the cross

Prayer

Gracious God, we are so grateful that you know our thoughts before they are even formed. In those times when we are beset by anxiety and confusion and our minds feel scattered, help us we pray, to gather them together and give them to you. Fill us with your peace, by the power of the Holy Spirit. Amen.

Your Space

THIRTY-SIX
Scripture - Ephesians 6:10-18

Finally, be strong in the Lord and in his mighty power. Put on the full armour of God, so that you can take your stand against the devil's schemes. For our struggle is not against flesh and blood, but against the rulers, against the authorities, against the powers of this dark world and against the spiritual forces of evil in the heavenly realms. Therefore put on the full armour of God, so that when the day of evil comes, you may be able to stand your ground, and after you have done everything, to stand. Stand firm then, with the belt of truth buckled around your waist, with the breastplate of righteousness in place, and with your feet fitted with the readiness that comes from the gospel of peace. In addition to all this, take up the shield of faith, with which you can extinguish all the flaming arrows of the evil one. Take the helmet of salvation and the sword of the Spirit, which is the word of God.

And pray in the Spirit on all occasions with all kinds of prayers and requests. With this in mind, be alert and always keep on praying for all the Lord's people.

Reflection

I (Karen) love this particular scripture. We are to equip ourselves the way a soldier would for battle, with all the various accoutrements necessary to keep us safe for the fight. But they are not the same - the breastplate is God's righteousness; the shield is faith. The shield that is our faith in God means that any fiery arrows aimed at us will bounce off - as long as we have remembered to use it. And remembering, being mindful of, our need for this armour - which takes time to put on - is what protects us.

"Our struggle is …. against the powers of this dark world and against the spiritual forces of evil in the heavenly realms." The helmet of salvation is very important. Our minds are often our biggest battleground, so to protect them from attack is important. Unfortunately, although much of the attack comes from the outside (the dark world), a great deal comes from our own unhelpful thoughts - what I often refer to as the whispers of the enemy.

The word 'stand' is repeated in this short text. In post-pandemic Britain where our economy is crippled, the political world is in turmoil, there is food poverty, and a fuel crisis, we can often feel paralysed. It's only by putting on the whole armour of God that we can be equipped for the fight.

The final instruction is to be alert- a very 'mindful' term and to pray about everything!

Mindful Thought

He said: "Listen, King Jehoshaphat and all who live in Judah and Jerusalem! This is what the Lord says to you: 'Do not be afraid or discouraged because of this vast army. For the battle is not yours, but God's."(2 Chronicles 20:15).

Mindful Action

Could you imagine symbolically putting on the 'armour of God' before beginning your day. How might you do this? Perhaps through practising some kind of spiritual discipline? Do you practice any spiritual disciplines? Yes - you do if you're on this devotional journey!

Prayer

Jesus, help us today to be strong in your mighty power and be alert to attacks, from within or outside, that might negatively impact our mental health or steal the peace you alone can give.

Remind us that we don't stand alone but that you are with us and would never abandon us.

Amen

Your Space

THIRTY-SEVEN
Scripture - Philippians 4:4-9

Rejoice in the Lord always. I will say it again: Rejoice! Let your gentleness be evident to all. The Lord is near. Do not be anxious about anything, but in every situation, by prayer and petition, with thanksgiving, present your requests to God. And the peace of God, which transcends all understanding, will guard your hearts and your minds in Christ Jesus.

Finally, brothers and sisters, whatever is true, whatever is noble, whatever is right, whatever is pure, whatever is lovely, whatever is admirable—if anything is excellent or praiseworthy—think about such things. Whatever you have learned or received or heard from me or seen in me—put it into practice. And the God of peace will be with you.

Reflection

This scripture exemplifies the Apostle Paul's practice of mindfulness of the presence of God.

He is shackled in a Roman prison. Humanly he has every reason to be anxious and upset, but he chooses to be mindful. He recognises the importance of showing delight and joy that God is with him and of praying/meditating. Our problems when shared - with a trusted friend or a paid therapist - begin to gain perspective and, often, lose their power to steal our peace. Prayer is having this conversation with God rather than ruminating upon it.

To experience 'The peace of God' is quite simply amazing. When, during meditation, my body has been flooded with oxytocin (which is the 'feel good' hormone that counteracts stress hormones in the body) this is how I would describe what happens to me.

The next practice, and that is the exact word Paul uses, is to <u>choose</u> his thoughts. The mind is our biggest battleground. We 'think' that we have no choice about what we think but paying attention to thoughts is a choice. Research suggests that a negative thought takes 3 seconds to register and to stick, yet a positive thought takes 12 seconds to register and then easily slides from our mind. It takes practice to challenge this hard wiring of the brain. The brain is subject to neuroplasticity so can be changed. We need to choose our thoughts wisely. In order to do this, first and foremost, we need to recognise that what we are doing is thinking. We are not our thoughts. If it is "true, noble, right" etc... then we can choose to think about it; if it is not then we can allow it to pass.

Mindful Thought

"Is what I am thinking helping or harming me?"[63]

Mindful Action

Recognise that what you are doing is thinking and that you do have the ability to choose whether you allow a thought to take hold and proliferate or allow it to pass. Choose helpful thoughts.

Prayer

Loving Lord, Give me a greater awareness of my thoughts today, I pray. Help me to recognise the whispers of the enemy who comes to steal, kill, and destroy. Guard my mind and my heart and keep me in your ways with my mind set on you.

Amen

---

[63] Lucy Hone (Ted talk *The three secrets of resilient people*) https://youtu.be/9-5SMpg7Q0k

Your Space

THIRTY-EIGHT
Scripture - Colossians 1:9b-14

Paul wrote to the people of Colossae:
...we have not ceased praying for you and asking that you may be filled with the knowledge of God's will in all spiritual wisdom and understanding, so that you may lead lives worthy of the Lord, fully pleasing to Him, as you bear fruit in every good work and as you grow in the knowledge of God. May you be made strong with all the strength that comes from His glorious power, and may you be prepared to endure everything with patience, while joyfully giving thanks to the Father, who has called us to share in the inheritance of the saints in the light. He has rescued us from the power of darkness and transferred us into the kingdom of His beloved Son, in whom we have redemption, the forgiveness of sins. [64]

Reflection

As we make space in our day to spend time with the Holy One, we receive these prayers that were prayed for the people of Colossae. The phrases in this section of St Paul's letter can become words to dwell on, asking the Holy Spirit to fulfil them in us. For example, you may want to synchronise your inbreath and outbreath with the words in each sentence;

• May our minds be filled with the knowledge of God's will, with insight into the ways and purposes of God, with understanding and discernment from the Holy Spirit.
• May we live the kind of lives that prove we belong to the Lord. May we please him in every way as we bear fruit, growing in our knowledge about God.
• May God strengthen us with his own great power, so that

---

[64] The Holy Bible, New Revised Standard Version Bible: Anglicised Edition. Copyright © 1989, 1995. Used by permission of the Division of Christian Education of the National Council of the Churches of Christ in the United States of America.

we will be patient and not give up when troubles come.

• May we joyfully thank God that he has enabled us to share in the inheritance of the saints.

• May we thank God that he has rescued us from the power of darkness and has brought us into the kingdom of his beloved Son, by whose death we have been set free and all our sins have been forgiven.

Mindful Thought

"We are cups, constantly and quietly being filled. The trick is, knowing how to tip ourselves over and let the beautiful stuff out."[65]

Mindful Action

When you face a difficult challenge today, pause to ask God for patience to get through, and later, pause to thank Him for His presence with you.

Prayer

Lord, we thank You that we can come into the present moment and breathe in Your presence with us. May we allow the Holy Spirit to transform and change our minds and hearts, so that we can see the good in everyone we meet and greet them as Jesus would. Amen.

---

[65] Ray Bradbury https://www.goodreads.com/quotes/1004-we-are-cups-constantly-and-quietly-being-filled-the-trick - accessed 5 Aug 22.

Your Space

THIRTY-NINE
Scripture - Colossians 3:5 and 3:15

Put to death whatever belongs to your earthly nature: sexual immorality, lust, evil desires and greed, which is idolatry.

Let the peace of Christ rule in your hearts, since as members of one body you were called to peace. And be thankful.

Reflection

We have deliberately juxtaposed these two verses for today's reflection, as indeed the Apostle Paul did (albeit with other verses between).

A key aspect of mindfulness is being awake and alert. If we are awake and alert then we notice, and can pay attention to, the very human emotions described in verse 5. We do this in order not to be overwhelmed or consumed by them. This way we can then choose our thoughts and, in so doing, we are enabled to mindfully, and by God's grace clothe ourselves with "compassion [including for ourselves], kindness, humility, gentleness and patience" (3:12) and the ultimate 'overall garment' …. "love" (3:14). This opens the door to the life-giving gift of the peace of Christ ruling our hearts and our lives.

Mindful Thought

How easy do we find it to let the peace of Christ rule in our hearts? During a conversation between Thich Nhat Hanh and Thomas Merton in 1966, the Buddhist monk said, "We don't teach meditation to young monks. They are not ready for it until they stop slamming doors."[66]

---

[66] https://theprayinglife.com/tag/thich-nhat-hanh/ - accessed 24 Jun 2022.

Mindful Action

Repressing or suppressing (pushing them down or away) feelings or emotions that we may be afraid or ashamed of can turn them into monsters. To put them to death we must first honestly acknowledge them. Accept them and recognise that they are just thoughts. In doing this you can then choose not to pursue the thought or allow it to proliferate. Allow it to pass. A simple yet effective technique is to greet the thought "Hello thought" and bid it farewell "Goodbye thought." It may sound silly but it's surprisingly effective! And now focus or meditate on the changeless peace-filled mind of Christ.

Prayer

May the peace of God, which passes all understanding, keep your heart and mind in the knowledge and love of God, and of his son, Jesus Christ our Lord. Amen.[67]

Your Space

---

[67] Taken from The Dismissal, *Common Worship,* (London: Church House Publishing, 2000) p 183.

FORTY

Scripture - 1 Peter 5:8-11

Be alert and of sober mind. Your enemy the devil prowls around like a roaring lion looking for someone to devour. Resist him, standing firm in the faith, because you know that the family of believers throughout the world is undergoing the same kind of sufferings.

And the God of all grace, who called you to his eternal glory in Christ, after you have suffered a little while, will himself restore you and make you strong, firm and steadfast. To him be the power for ever and ever. Amen.

Reflection

"Be alert" Peter tells us, and of "sober mind." For alert we might read 'awake' or 'aware.' What comes to your mind when you read that? For 'sober' most people would think of the opposite of drunk - but actually to be sober minded means to be sensible and wise. And to do those things is to be mindful.

The biggest battleground we face is that of our own minds. And all that is needed for that to happen is for us to allow the seeds of a thought to take root and to grow; to be 'devoured' by unhelpful imaginings. We resist, not by denying or pushing such thoughts under the carpet, but by acknowledging and being alert to the thoughts which threaten to steal our peace and by noticing the stories we tell ourselves. Peter seeks to reassure us by reminding us that we are not on our own in this - the family of believers throughout the world suffers in the same way. When he speaks of the whole world suffering this is because the people he's writing to were early members of the Jerusalem church which has been scattered all over what is now modern-day Turkey, because of persecution. But actually, the whole world suffers the same way. I suggest though that a major difference between those with and without faith is the gift of the knowledge of the presence of God in the present moment, whatever the circumstances. And, through prayer, we can place our troubled thoughts at the foot of the cross. We can breathe in God's peace. And we can be restored.

Mindful Thought

"The thief comes only to steal and kill and destroy; I have come that they may have life and have it to the full." (John 10 v10).

Mindful Action

If you are feeling anxious or upset (or even if you aren't) take a moment to recognise that you are thinking (we have somewhere between 60 and 80,000 thoughts a day). Imagine that you are outside of your body looking at the thought. The thought isn't you. Now gently cup the thought in your hands and place it at the foot of the cross. Take a couple of breaths. Breathing in through the nose, imagine being filled with God's peace and breathe out any remaining anxiety through your mouth.

Prayer

In your suffering may the God of all grace, who called you to his eternal glory in Christ, restore you and make you strong, firm, and steadfast. To him be the power for ever and ever. Amen. (1 Peter 5:10)

Your Space

Suggested Reading

BABBS, L., *Into God's presence: Listening to God through prayer and meditation* (Michigan: Zondervan, 2005).

BANE, P & Litton, M., *In the Presence of Jesus. A 40-Day Guide to the Intimacy with God You've Always Wanted.* (Illinois: Tyndale House Publishers, 2021)

BELL, R., *How to be here,* (New York: HarperCollins Publishers, 2017)

CASEY, M., *Sacred reading*, (Liguori, Mo.: Liguori/Triumph 2008).

COE, J.H., and STROBEL, K.C., ed. *Embracing Contemplation* (Strobel IVP Academic, 2019).

COLLICUTT, J., BRETHERTON, R., BRICKMAN, J., *Being Mindful, Being Christian* (Chicago: Lion Hudson 2016).
DRAPER, B., Soulfulness (Hodder & Stoughton Canada 2020).

FRUEHWIRTH, G., *Words for Silence: A Year of Contemplative Meditations* (SPCK, 2008)

MARIONA, J. and WILBER, K., *Putting on the mind of Christ* (Newburyport: Hampton Roads Publishing 201).

LAIRD, M., *Into the Silent Land* (London: DLT, 2006).

LAMBERT, S., *A Book of Sparks: A Study in Christian MindFullness* (Watford: Instant Apostle, 2014).

___, *Putting on the wakeful one* (Watford: Instant Apostle, 2016).

LAWRENCE, BR., Lawrence, Br., *The Practice of the presence of God* (Mockingbird Classics, 2015).

MAIN, J., *Being Present Now: Door to Silence* (Norwich: Canterbury Press, 2006).

___, *The Heart of Creation* (London: DLT, 1988).

NOUWEN, H.J.M., *The Way of the Heart* (New York: Harper Collins, 1981).

ODEN, AMY G., *Right Here, Right Now: The Practice of Christian Mindfulness* (Nashville: Abingdon Press, 2017).

OPENSHAW, K and EDMONDSON, C. *Mindfulness as Mission Gift* (Fresh Expressions, 2022)

REYNOLDS, S., *Living with the Mind of Christ* (Minneapolis, Minnesota: Augsburg Books 2020).

ROHR, R., *Falling Upward: A Spirituality for the Two Halves of Life* (SPCK, 2012).

STEAD, T., *Mindfulness and Christian Spirituality-Making Space for God* (London: SPCK, 2016).

___, *See, Love, Be: Mindfulness and the Spiritual Life: a practical eight-week guide* (London, SPCK, 2018).

___, *Mindfulness and Prayer* (Cambridge: Grove Books Ltd, 2016).

THOMAS, G., *Sacred Pathways* (Grand Rapids, Mich: Zondervan 2000).

WELCH, S., n.d. *How to be a Mindful Christian*. (Norwich, Canterbury Press, 2016)

WILLIAMS, M. and PENMAN, d., *Mindfulness: A Practical Guide to Finding Peace in a Frantic World* (London, Piatkus 2011).

ABOUT THE AUTHORS

Chris Edmondson

Chris has worked in a variety of parish and diocesan posts in the Church of England, as well as having been Warden of Lee Abbey, Devon from 2002 to 2008. Prior to his retirement in 2016, Chris was Bishop of Bolton for eight years in the Diocese of Manchester. During that time, he chaired the Manchester Fresh Expressions Area Strategy Team, and was also Vice Chair of the National Fresh Expressions Board. Chris has been the Chair of the Council of Scargill House since 2009 and is the author of two books on leadership. Having been ordained for almost 50 years, Chris continues to be committed to seeing the Gospel freshly expressed in each new generation. As an outworking of this he is involved in a local fresh expression of church. He is also Chaplain for Yorkshire Cricket Club.

Karen Openshaw

Karen runs a consultancy which provides a listening service for organisations and individuals, drawing on the 'toolbox' of her eclectic mix of counselling, mentoring, chaplaincy, and coaching training. She offers coaching for business owners and those with leadership responsibilities. Karen delivers workshops in both Christian and secular organisations, introducing people to the concept of mindfulness. She developed a fresh expression of church in 2012 at the Oasis Academy, Media City UK in Salford, where she was chaplain. She was a board Director for Fresh Expressions Ltd from 2017-2020. She now leads a local fresh expression called 'WonderWalkers', combining her passion for mindfulness, walking and love of God. She is co-author, along with Chris, of Mindfulness as Mission Gift. www.karenopenshaw.co.uk

ABOUT THE CONTRIBUTORS

Paul Bane

Paul is the founder of Mindful Christianity, an online community helping people discover the lost contemplative and meditative tradition of practising the presence of Jesus in our daily lives. Founded in 2015, Mindful Christianity now reaches over a million people a day, and its message has connected with faith leaders in every denomination of Christianity, as well as mental health professionals and counselling organisations. Paul is the retired senior pastor of New Hope Community Church in Brentwood, Tennessee. He and his wife, Cathy, have two grown children and six granddaughters. https://mindfulchristianitytoday.com

Martin Grindrod

Martin's seeds of interest in Eastern philosophy/meditation were first sown in martial arts practice. He is a Mindfulness Based Transformational coach, accredited mindfulness teacher, and has trained extensively in cognitive therapy which he incorporates into his mindfulness programmes.

Martin is a practising Christian and has found that his practise of mindfulness has brought him closer to God and allowed him to connect with creation at a deeper level. It also helps him cope with the pain and anxiety of severe osteoarthritis, which led to him having a total hip replacement at the age of 44, as well as the highs and lows of daily living.

He teaches mindfulness both 1:1 and in group settings, either in-person, or via Zoom. (Karen is one of his former students). www.inspireevolution.co.uk

Richard H H Johnston

Rich Johnston is the founder of Christian Mindfulness and Mindful Church. He is one of the founding leaders of the UK National Mindfulness Day for Christians, the International Christian Mindfulness Conference, and the author of several books on mindfulness. He has completed the UK Mindfulness Association Practitioner Certificate and Mindfulness Association Foundation Course.
https://christianmindfulness.co.uk

Shaun Lambert

Rev Dr Shaun Lambert is a Baptist Minister, author psychotherapist, and mindfulness researcher, married with two children and a dog called Coco. Having recently been part of the community at Scargill House in Yorkshire, a retreat centre and international community, he continues to have regular involvement there. Shaun is looking to explore mindful church/mindful community for young people in the light of the epidemic of mental health distress amongst young people as well as a turn to spirituality in that generation. He has experienced anxiety, stress, and burnout and is very interested in helping others move into wellbeing out of distress. https://shaunlambert.co.uk

Belinda Norrington

A mindfulness teacher and researcher in the UK, currently studying for an MSc in Mindfulness and Compassion. She recently spent two years working part-time in a pastoral role for a local church, collaboratively exploring the overlap between wellbeing and faith, creating courses and contemplative practice spaces within a church context. She is a regular contributor to The Mind and Soul Foundation as well as a guest on various media outlets where she talks about contemplative practices and wellbeing.
https://www.wildacrewellbeing.co.uk

Amy Oden

Born and raised on the prairies of Oklahoma, Dr Amy Oden has found her spiritual home under the wide-open sky. Her passion is to introduce spiritual practices that can ground and nourish lives that follow Jesus in the world. Amy teaches theology, history of Christianity and spiritual formation, walking with students in their learning. https://www.amyoden.com

Stephen Radley

Rev Stephen is an Anglican priest and professional photographer. A military veteran, he found healing from his military experiences through photography and in 2021 he was awarded the Amateur Photographer Magazine Unsung Hero Award.

Growing up in the Lake District Stephen has a love of the outdoors, especially fell walking, and is a keen sailor who sails with Sailability alongside people with disabilities. He is trained in counselling as well as being a doctoral student, researching healing after trauma through photography, with an MSc in Psychiatry & War. He suffered from both depression, anxiety and moral injury, the latter following his last deployment to Afghanistan. Stephen's experience of war left him with a passion to help people find peace by seeing in new ways. This desire saw him pioneer a new direction in his ministry, using image to promote resilience and build relationships through his organisation, Soulful Vision, which brings together study and personal experience. He leads retreats and workshops across the UK and Ireland and in 2000, he also joined the RAF Chaplains branch. https://www.soulfulvision.uk

Beverley Walker

Bev is a retired teacher from Wiltshire. Brought up as an

Anglican, she is now a Methodist and supports blended services at her church as a 'Digital Steward', keeping in touch with the online congregation. After a diagnosis of a chronic illness, Bev became interested in mindfulness as a way of living life to the full and in the present moment. During the lockdown of 2020 Bev completed the Associated Certificate in Christian Mindfulness, and now teaches NHS courses for people with chronic pain and is working towards a similar qualification in Christian contemplation. Bev regularly leads Mindful Church, a recently formed online 'fresh expression' focussed on relationship with Jesus Christ, relationship with one another and the value and importance of self-care to improve mental health.

Printed in Great Britain
by Amazon

11746813R00070